THE BOOK OF THE
BIZARRE

FREAKY FACTS & STRANGE STORIES

VARLA VENTURA

⚲ WEISERBOOKS
San Francisco, CA / Newburyport, MA

FOR THE WICKED, THE WEARY,
AND THE LOVERS OF THE STRANGE

First published in 2008 by
Red Wheel/Weiser, LLC
With offices at:
500 Third Street, Suite 230
San Francisco, CA 94107
www.redwheelweiser.com

ISBN: 978-1-57863-437-8
Library of Congress Cataloging-in-Publication Data is available upon request.

Cover and text design by Sara Gillingham.
Typeset in Antihistory, Toronto Gothic, and Rough Egyptienne.
Cover illustrations © Miss Mary, LLC.
Text illustrations on pages 104, 129, 151, 168, 173, 234, 253 © The Pepin Press. All
other illustrations © Miss Mary, LLC.

Printed in Canada
TCP
10 9 8 7 6 5 4 3 2 1

 CONTENTS

1. SOMETHING WICKED

⟨ THE MAGICAL SKULL OF DOOM ⟩

Very few objects have engendered as much controversy or imaginative conjecture as the Magical Skull of Doom, a crystal skull life size in its circumference and likeness to the human head. Shrouded in mysterious and unknown origins, there are countless tales of strange phenomena associated with it. Some believe it is haunted, others believe it is cursed, and still others believe it is of extraterrestrial origin.

As legend has it, the skull first turned up in the 1920s under an altar in the archaeological dig of the ruins of Lubaantun, the great Mayan city in what is now known as Belize. Some of the greatest arguments occur over whether or not the Magical Skull of Doom is pre-Columbian. While other crystal skulls have been discovered in Central American ruins, none can match the Skull of Doom for its perfection of craftsmanship and likeness to a real skull. Perhaps the biggest mystery of all is that the crystal from which the skull was carved appears to be derived only from California, not the Mayan territory.

Frederick Mitchell Hedges, one of the archaeologists who was present at the discovery, is rumored to have planted it on the occasion of his adopted daughter Ann's birthday, the day of the skull's discovery. It has also been suggested that the skull was never in Lubaantun. Nevertheless, Hedges proclaimed that the skull was "used by the high priest of the Maya to concentrate on and will death," that it was "the embodiment of all evil," or that people who scoffed at the skull have died or "have been stricken and become seriously ill." Hedges also attributed to the large hunk of crystal the moniker of "the Skull of Doom" and greatly aided in the swirl of rumors, mist, and myth that has continued to enshroud it.

Frank Dortland, a highly reputable art restorer and one of the later owners of the skull, kept and studied the Magical Skull of Doom. Dortland swore that the skull gave off an "elusive perfume," that it seemed to emanate a sound similar to bells chiming, and that it could change color at will. He also claimed that it sometimes was filled with ever-changing, cloudy images and at other times it contained crystal-clear images of temples, mountains, and myriad other striking scenes. Other folks who observed the skull when it was under Dortland's watch said a hazy aura would occasionally enshroud it. Still stranger are the reports of physiological phenomena, such as a quickening of the pulse, muscle spasms in the legs and arms, and even eye twitching, affecting people who were near the skull.

Maybe people are fascinated with the Magical Skull of Doom because it is simple in its inherent magnificence. It looks like it was formed whole, and it bears nearly no sign of tool marks. The artist who created this skull was a master of the highest order—the handiwork is nothing short of spectacular. Just polishing the skull would have been a labor of some years. The proverbial icing on the cake is especially fascinating: the skull is crafted in such a way that light collects and refracts in the eye sockets, causing them to emit an eerie glow.

⟨ THE TRANSYLVANIAN TABLETS ⟩

In 1961 archaeologists digging into a prehistoric mound in the Transylvanian village of Tartaria made a startling discovery—several small clay tablets with bizarre inscriptions on them. Some believed the inscriptions to be sigils or magical signs, and others believed that they were important documents left behind for the singular purpose of being found—time capsules, perhaps. Using the modern method of carbon dating, the objects' origin was placed at around 4000 B.C. The writing was believed to be of Mesopotamian origin, specifically Sumerian, the first written language. Could this discovery mean the origins of writing began in the wild backwoods of Transylvania?

The three tablets were found in the lowest layer of the dig. They were in a sacrificial pit within a burial mound, and the pit also contained some scattered human bones. The bones bore symbols quite similar to the inscriptions on the tablets; the symbols were both from Sumer and from the highly advanced Minoan civilizations of Crete. But if the carbon dating is accurate, the tablets were made by a primitive Stone Age agricultural tribe known as the Vinca. The Vinca predated Sumerian writing by one millennium and the Minoan writing by two thousand years. Most scholars believe that the inscriptions were magical ciphers—spells and secret codes of this ancient farming tribe. The hash marks, swirls, *x*'s, and shapes on the three tablets cast a spell over mystery lovers, too.

⟨ STONEHENGE ⟩

Built over four thousand years ago, Stonehenge, the massive stone monument that sits on the Salisbury Plain of England, is shrouded in mystery and legend. Was it constructed as an ancient calendar and used to predict astrological events or seasonal changes? Or was it a place of worship, a spiritual temple built to honor the deities of its makers?

The purpose of this spectacular man-made rock formation has been studied and debated for centuries. Just as bewildering is the question of how Stonehenge was created. Some of the stones used are believed to have come from hundreds of miles away. How were these rocks, some weighing up to four tons, transported such a distance in an era before the invention of the wheel? No one knows for sure.

And no one knows for sure *who* built Stonehenge. There are many supernatural and mystical theories, though none have ever been proven. Some believe Stonehenge was the creation of aliens, while others claim that the sorcerer Merlin used his magical powers to move the stones across the land and sea. One legend even tells of the devil creating Stonehenge as part of a bizarre riddle he concocted to toy with local villagers.

⊰ STONE'S PUBLIC HOUSE ⊱

Numerous stories of ghostly encounters surround Stone's Public House in Ashland, Massachusetts. The inn and pub was built in 1834 by John Stone and still serves as a restaurant and pub today.

The assistant manager of Stone's tells a tale of being alone in the pub one night, finishing up the day's duties, and having a sudden feeling of terror. Then a handful of birdseed fell through holes in the ceiling, rattling to his newly mopped floor. Other staffers report water faucets turning on by themselves, and numerous patrons say they have felt someone tapping on their shoulder only to find no one behind them when they turn around.

A noted hypnotist and parapsychologist, Ralph Bibbo, visited the inn numerous times and says that there are at least six, possibly seven, different ghosts that dwell there. Bibbo says that Stone himself accidentally killed a boarder in 1845 and tried to cover up the murder. The other spirits were accomplices or witnesses to Stone's crime. Having sworn to keep Stone's crime a secret while they were alive, they are still bound to the pub in death.

⟨ THE TOWER OF LONDON ⟩

The Tower of London is perhaps the most infamous haunted dwelling in history. Built over a two-hundred-year period beginning in the early eleventh century, the complex is seen as an architectural wonder, having over twenty towers and occupying over eighteen acres of land.

The Tower of London was used as by English monarchs as a prison, and it has housed some of Britain's most notorious of criminals. Murderers and traitors to the crown were locked up in one of its many towers to await execution, and those prisoners who were sentenced to death were beheaded within the Tower's very walls. Many of those who were beheaded are said to haunt the Tower to this day. Lady Jane Grey, who held the throne for only nine days in 1554 before being executed in the Tower, is said to appear every year on the day of her death, holding her own head beneath her arm.

Two other murdered queens, Anne Boleyn and Katherine Howard, both wives of Henry the VIII, also are said to appear within the Tower as two headless figures surrounded by a supernatural glow. Katherine has even be seen and heard wandering the halls and begging for mercy as she did on the day of her execution.

One of the Tower's most gruesome murders was of the Countess of Salisbury. As her head was placed on the executioner's block, she panicked and tried to run. The executioner chased her down and hacked her to death with his axe. It is said that the spirits of the countess and her executioner appear and reenact her brutal murder.

Of all the ghostly sightings in the Tower of London, the most disturbing are the apparitions of two small boys walking along the hallways hand in hand. These boys are believed to be the sons and heirs of King Edward V. Edward's brother Richard, the duke of Gloucester, placed his nephews in the Tower after King Edward's death. He later smothered the two princes in their sleep, so that he could claim the king's throne for himself.

<hr/>

"It's fascinating to think that all around us there's an invisible world we can't even see. I'm speaking, of course, of the World of the Invisible Scary Skeletons." —JACK HANDY

<hr/>

⟨ A GHOST TO BE ⟩

What manner of death creates a ghost? While many ghosts may stay on after their passing because they are fond of a place (or person), most hauntings are attributed to some kind of disruptive death. Leslie Rule describes these as "ghost makers" in her book *Coast to Coast Ghosts*:

1. Murder. Unsolved killings especially. Ghost often moves on once the murder is solved.
2. Suicide. Torment equals a soul bound to earth.

3. Accidents. Sudden deaths have more hauntings attached to them than deaths of natural causes.
4. Broken hearts. Those who die mourning are often the source of ghostly activity.
5. Greed. A preoccupation with land or money in life can be carried into the beyond.
6. Lack of proper burial or desecration of grave site.

> "FROM THE BODY OF ONE GUILTY DEED A THOUSAND GHOSTLY FEARS AND HAUNTING THOUGHTS PROCEED." —WILLIAM WORDSWORTH

⊰ KING'S TAVERN, NATCHEZ, MISSISSIPPI ⊱

The story of the ghosts at King's Tavern in Natchez, Mississippi, dates back to the late 1700s, when a woman named Madeline, the mistress of Richard King, was murdered by King's jealous wife. For more than 200 years, the tavern's patrons have reported hauntings, including the ghost of a woman standing in front of them, angrily poised with hands on her hips.

In the 1930s, the skeleton of a woman was discovered sealed in a brick fireplace, a dagger in her chest.

⟨ SILAS OF KENNEBUNK ⟩

The Kennebunk Inn in Kennebunkport, Maine is reputed to be haunted by a friendly ghost named Silas. Among Silas's tricks are levitating glasses and throwing beer mugs.

⟨ REBECCA DORRINGTON'S FATAL FALL ⟩

In the High Sierra of California, among the pines and fresh mountain air, the little town of Dorrington is home to the Dorrington Hotel. The town is named after Rebecca Dorrington, who died in a fatal fall down a flight of stairs in the hotel in 1870. Today's hotel guests report banging doors, flashing lights, and furniture shifting. Some have even claimed to witness a phantom re-creation of Rebecca's fatal fall.

⟨ HAUNTED? A CHECKLIST ⟩

Here are six telltale signs that your house may be haunted, especially if any of the signs occur repeatedly:

1. Pets react with seemingly out-of-place growls, barks, or hisses to things no one else can see.
2. Household members have repeated nightmares.

3. Objects disappear, often to reappear somewhere else after some time. For example, a young woman living in an old railroad flat in Santa Fe has come home to find her ghost had moved or turned over her sugar bowl on numerous occasions.

4. Electrical appliances turn on or off by themselves. Faucets or toilets run or flush themselves.

5. The building has inexplicable cold drafts or cold spots.

6. Inhabitants hear footsteps, taps on walls or windows, and voices that cannot be attributed to other living people or sources in the house.

> "WHERE'ER WE TREAD 'TIS HAUNTED, HOLY GROUND." —LORD BYRON

NEW ENGLAND GHOST
►➤ AS TOLD BY RAYMOND BUCKLAND ◄◄

I first came to the United States in 1962. I lived on Long Island, New York, and then, about ten years later, moved up to live on the shores of Lake Winnepesaukee, New Hampshire. My wife and I purchased a house there, at Weirs Beach.

The house was built circa 1825. It was a beautiful two-story with an attached ell barn, stable, and outbuildings, set on a couple of acres. Right from the start we felt very comfortable and very welcomed in the house. It had a very large living room with a wonderful beamed ceiling. The room ran the length of the house on the west side. A staircase went up the center of the house; the front door was at its base, and there were four bedrooms above. On the east side of the house was the kitchen and my study. My study had two windows looking out to the front and one looking to the side. A later addition was a screened-in porch that ran across the full front of the house. The door at the east end of this porch opened onto a paved path leading to the garage and the driveway.

We quickly came to realize that the house was haunted. While we sat downstairs in the living room, we frequently heard footsteps walking about in the bedrooms. I particularly remember one time when the footsteps walked across the room above (my elder son's front bedroom) and then started down the stairs. My wife and I were sitting in the living room, and we both turned to see who had come down, since neither of my sons was home; we expected the person to come around the corner from the foot of the stairs into the living room. But no one came. The footsteps had stopped at the bottom of the stairs. I got up out of my chair and went to look. There was no one there; the staircase was empty.

On another occasion my wife's grandmother was staying with us, sleeping in my elder son's bedroom. One morning she came down to breakfast and reported a nighttime visitor. She said that she had awakened in the middle of the night to find a woman standing at the foot of her bed. There was a night-light in the room, and she could see that the woman was wearing a long blue dress. The figure studied her for a few moments and then turned and simply disappeared, fading away to nothing.

I saw a figure myself, once. I was in my study when I heard the screen door bang and looked up to glimpse a man crossing the porch to go to the front door. As I got up from my desk, I expected to hear the front doorbell ring, but it didn't. I went and opened the door and looked out. There was no one there. The porch was empty. There was no one outside or anywhere in the driveway. The screen door invariably squeaked when opened, but I didn't hear it squeak on this occasion.

We lived in the house for almost five years and became accustomed to our ghosts. They were in no way malevolent. We were sorry to say good-bye to them when we eventually sold the house and moved away.

"Nothing beats a haunted moonlit night on All Hallows Eve…And on this fatal night, at this witching time, the starless sky laments black and unmoving. The somber hues of an ominous, dark forest are suddenly illuminated under the emerging face of the full moon." —KIM ELIZABETH

⊰ NOT ALL HAUNTS ARE OLD ⊱

Brad Steiger's *Real Ghosts, Restless Spirits, and Haunted Places* is chock full of fantastically frightening true tales of terror. Among them is the story of a woman and her husband who moved into a house in 1992, when the house was just eleven years old. Not long after moving in, the woman began to hear someone walking in her upstairs hallway. Convinced it was her son sneaking out, she would go upstairs to check on him and find him sleeping soundly in bed. At first, she did not speak of the footsteps, not even to her husband and son. Then the footsteps increased in frequency and changed location, including coming into her bedroom. It didn't take her long to learn from her husband that he, too, was hearing many strange noises, particularly when he was home alone during the brightness of day. In the first month of living there, she told author Steiger that they went through at least one hundred lightbulbs; lights were constantly blowing out all throughout the house.

The woman said the noises had begun just after the family had moved in—when she'd hung an old lead mirror, left behind by the previous owners, in the hallway opposite her son's room. Only when she got rid of the mirror did the noises stop.

⟨ ANIMAL APPARITIONS ⟩

Not only do animals sense ghosts, but animals also can be ghosts. For example:

➤ Actor Rudolph Valentino's Great Dane, Kabar, is reported to haunt his former owner's gravesite.

➤ In Port Tabacco, Maryland, there is a bloodstained rock known to locals as Peddler's Rock. It is said to be home to the Blue Dog, who guards his dead master's buried treasure.

➤ In Casper, Wyoming, ranchers have long reported the image of a white steed galloping across the area known as Rattlesnake Range. This horse was known as White Devil when he was alive, due to his reputation for fiercely defending himself and other horses against the mighty lasso.

In Reading, Pennsylvania, the ghosts of Mrs. Bissinger and her children still roam an area near the Union Lock Canal where she drowned herself (and her children) in 1875. Visitors to this area often report being overwhelmed by a sad and horrific energy.

⊰ A FOND FAREWELL ⊱

Dana was the youngest of four kids, living in an old Victorian house in the Minnesota suburbs. Her grandfather, who lived in the same town as she did, was sick in the hospital, but Dana was too young to really know what was going on or that he was dying. One day while her mother was at the hospital, Dana came walking down the grand staircase in her house. To her surprise, she saw her grandfather walking up toward her, looking healthy and happy. "I wanted to say good-bye, Dana, and I love you very much," he said and continued up the stairs. Delighted, the child raced into the kitchen to tell her mother that Grandpa was all better and that he'd come over for a visit. But her mother had just returned from the hospital with some bad news—her grandfather had passed away earlier that afternoon.

※※※※※※※※※※※※※※※※※※※※※※※※※※※※※※※※※※※※

Have you seen a ghost? It is possible that you have and just didn't know what to look for. If the figure you saw was unusually pale, disappeared after an instant, ignored you when you spoke or called out, appeared in an odd place, or was dressed inappropriately (often of another era), perhaps you have seen a ghost. (Of course, many of these characteristics could describe some of your relatives as well.)

※※※※※※※※※※※※※※※※※※※※※※※※※※※※※※※※※※※※

THE HAUNTED BOAT HOUSE
▶➤ AS TOLD BY CHRIS WARD ◀◀

It was late October 2004, and as part of a unique archaeological project along the Drakes Bay bluff on the Point Reyes National Seashore in Northern California, our five-person team was given accommodation at the restored Drakes Bay Lifesaving Station, otherwise known as the Boat House.

The Boat House, a National Historic Landmark, is an impressive building overlooking the waters of Drakes Bay. As the park official led us on our initial tour of the building, I could not help but notice a creeping feeling that seemed to hang around. These sensations increased when we were brought into the Boat Room. The Boat Room houses a now-decommissioned lifeboat, the first motorized lifeboat north of San Francisco Bay. The lifeboat had been used in countless rescue missions from 1953 to 1965, covering the extent of the Northern California coastline from Drakes Bay north to Humboldt Bay. I had to wonder why such a unique historic relic was shut away in this room. It was resting half on the ground, half off, teetering on an old wooden sawhorse. When I inquired, the park official responded with this story.

On a stormy Thanksgiving eve in 1960, the Coast Guard team at Drakes Bay was alerted to a cry for help from a fishing boat that appeared to be in distress north of Fort Bragg. A well-trained and competent crew, they quickly responded. A two-person crew launched the lifeboat into the dark night (no easy task) and headed

north to Fort Bragg through blinding rain and turbu-
lent seas. The experienced seamen made their way up
the rocky and treacherous coast and successfully towed
the fishing boat to shore just outside of Fort Bragg. They
then reportedly headed south to Drakes Bay. The crew
members never returned to the Boat House.

The following morning a search party headed to the
Boat House, only to discover a horrific sight. The lifeboat had run aground not more than 150 yards from its
berth at the Boat House. The engine and propeller were
still churning. Yet neither member of the crew was in
sight. Although the lifeboat had traveled hundreds of
miles in the most adverse of conditions and had returned to the very bay from whence it had launched,
there was no sign of either seaman. Their bodies were
never found. Shortly thereafter, the Boat House was de-
commissioned and the lifeboat locked away.

For some twenty years, the lifeboat sat in its home,
until the National Park Service created the Point Reyes
National Seashore, and the historic Boat House and
lifeboat therein became part of a lengthy restoration
process. The park service restored the lifeboat to its
former glory, intending to take it back out into the bay
for special occasions. At last the day came for the boat
to be launched again into the salty waters. Reporters

and park supporters gathered round to view the lifeboat, which was supported on a carriage of two wooden sawhorses. Just at the moment of rechristening, the lifeboat lurched forward and crashed down, smashing one of the sawhorses and damaging the keel of the boat extensively. The boat would not again touch the waters of Drakes Bay, and it remains exactly where it fell, half on and half off the ground.

For four nights in late October, after long days of archaeological work, our five-person crew returned to the Boat House for a night's sleep. Yet these nights were anything but restful. Each member of our crew reported strange happenings and unexplained sounds. Mysterious footsteps creaked down the corridor outside the Captain's Room, when all members of our team were accounted for. Things slammed to the floor in the Boat Room—things that had been fastened tightly to the wall the night before. One of our crew members repeatedly said that there was somebody looking through the shelves in the kitchen, where she saw shadows. This sight was enough to scare her from her luxurious room downstairs to the bunks upstairs where the rest of us lodged.

A lunar eclipse, the shortened days and long nights of late October, a brewing storm, a boat house that rests three-quarters of the way over the murky waters of the bay—even a team of rational scientists could not help but feel that there was something decidedly haunted about the Boat House.

<hr>

"It is an odd thing, but every one who disappears is said to be seen in San Francisco. It must be a delightful city, and possess all the attractions of the next world."
—OSCAR WILDE

<hr>

BIZARRE HAPPENINGS IN PORTLAND
▶▶ AS TOLD BY ALIX BENEDICT ◀◀

A friend of mine had purchased a house in Portland, Oregon, and was just completing a rather extensive renovation. One of the men who was working on the house was also staying there, despite the raw conditions. Throughout the period of time he was living there, he had numerous strange experiences. Doors slammed and then creaked open, and he had a constant feeling of being watched. The wires that had been rigged into light sockets and outlets were ripped clean, over and over. Painters reported open cans of paint had been turned upside down without a drop spilled, only for paint to go all over the floor when they attempted to move the can. My friend, the owner, had purchased a set of spiral stairs from an auction. The metal stairs had once been in the local jailhouse and were used by prisoners. Later, the man living in the house said that nothing happened until after they had installed the stairs.

When the renovation was nearly complete, I was hired to clean up and put the finishing touches on the place. One evening, I was at the house, working late. The owner was upstairs asleep, and I was in the basement with my headphones on. It was pretty late, at least 10 or 11 P.M. I had repeatedly felt something like a crawling sensation in my hair, but attributed it to spiders or dust, as the house was still in a bit of disarray. But then I felt and saw something that I knew was no spider! I was working in front of a bank of windows, cleaning them and scraping away the paint that had gotten on to the glass. As it was light inside but dark outside, the windows were a bit like a mirror. I felt something like a tug on a piece of my hair, and I looked at my reflection in the window. I actually saw a piece of my hair move up and away from my head, as if someone were standing behind me and pulling at it. I was dumbstruck and actually froze with shock. I stood there for what felt like several minutes, but was probably just a few seconds, and then promptly bolted upstairs and woke up the owner. I have lived in a few haunted places, but watching my hair move of its own accord was decidedly unnerving.

The owner and I did some historical research on the place and discovered that two people had died there in the past. One was a little old lady, who died of natural causes. The other was a local sheriff, who shot and killed himself in the house. We all came to suspect he was our ghost, especially because the stairs from the county jail seemed to trigger the start of all of the spooky and strange activity.

"Then away out in the woods I heard that kind of a sound that a ghost makes when it wants to tell about something that's on its mind and can't make itself understood, and so can't rest easy in its grave, and has to go about that way every night grieving." —MARK TWAIN

⊰ THE FLYING DUTCHMAN ⊱

A seventeenth-century Dutch merchant vessel, *The Flying Dutchman*, and her phantoms are legendary. The ship ran into trouble around the dangerous Cape of Good Hope in South Africa. Accounts of what exactly happened vary: some say Captain Hendrick van der Decken refused to seek shelter in the harbor, others say it was impossible to do so because of the weather. Regardless, *The Flying Dutchman* sank, but it hardly disappeared. Since the 1800s there have been sightings of a phantom ship that will sometimes pull alongside other ships, but the ghost ship is most often seen from the lighthouse point. Among the witnesses over the years were England's King George V and several famous authors.

THE GHOSTS OF NEVADA COUNTY, CALIFORNIA

⊰ A LITTLE HAUNTED HOTEL ON THE CORNER ⊱

In the historic town of Nevada City, California, high in the Sierra foothills, on the corner of Broad and Pine streets, there is a small hotel with a big history. Owner Katie Bennett, who bought the US Hotel in 2002, has heard strange noises and mysterious sounds regularly.

And so have her patrons. The odd occurrences include knocking noises, steps that sound like someone is right outside your door, and lights that flicker on and off. The most common thing Bennett hears is laughter, accompanied by music and footsteps as if someone is dancing. So it was no surprise to her when a team of paranormal investigators caught the sound of laughter and footsteps on tape. The recordings included a man calling out for someone named Olga, the sound of boots on hardwood floors, and popping and knocking noises. Visit *www.norcalghosthunters.com*, click on EVPs (electronic voice phenomena) and links, and then scroll down to "US Hotel B&B EVP Link" to hear the evidence for yourself.

━━━━▶⤻ A GHOSTLY IMAGE ⤻◀━━━━

In January of 2007 *The Union*, the local paper for Nevada County, California, reported that a ghostly face had appeared in a photograph. The photo had been taken of the historic Skidmore House, one of a dozen or so original homes still standing in North Bloomfield, a mining town that is now part of the Malakoff Diggins State Historic Park. Sonny Lopez, the park's maintenance mechanic, had moved to the park in July of 2006. He and his wife wanted window treatments that had an old-time feel, and so one afternoon Lopez took several photographs of Skidmore House and its windows. Later, when he went home to show the photos to his wife, he noticed that the otherwise empty home was perhaps not so empty. In one of the photos was a figure that looked like a woman with long hair, pulling back the curtain and looking back out at him. You can view the photograph yourself in *The Union*'s online archives at *www.theunion.com*. Do a search for "ghostly photographs" and see what appears.

▶❯ THE GHOST IN THE FLAME ❮◀

Originally built as a firehouse, a necessary building in a gold-rush town of shacks and temporary structures, the Fire House No. 2 in Nevada City, California, is now a historical museum. Visitors and employees alike have reported hearing footsteps in an otherwise empty room, as well as feeling sudden temperature changes, cold spots, and a general "thickening" of the atmosphere. Some witnesses claim to have seen the ghost of a Victorian woman, who searches through cabinets, and a female piano player from a nearby whorehouse. A few visitors have even sighted a group of Chinese men standing around a shrine, a testimony to the Chinese population that contributed to Nevada City's early growth.

A PARALYZING NIGHT
►►❯ AS TOLD BY GIOVANNI GALATI ❮◄◄

In the mid-1980s in Hanover, Germany, my family owned a large apartment house where my parents, brothers, I, and other employees of the restaurant my father owned would rent rooms. Many of the residents reported ghostly sightings and encounters. Some employees refused to stay. But I was the skeptic—until one night.

I arrived home late after work, close to one in the morning, and fell fast asleep. A few hours later, probably around four or five, I awoke suddenly, my eyes wide open. At this moment, I heard the key turn in the lock to my front door. Instinctively, I tried to get up to see who it could be. I lived alone and thought I had the only key to the apartment. But I was completely paralyzed. I could not move—not my fingers, my toes, nor even my head—to see who could be there.

As I lay there struggling with the inability to move, I heard footsteps go through the hall and into the kitchen, echoing across the wooden floors. I then heard the handle of my bedroom door begin to turn. I could hear someone or something come in the door and stand next to my bed, looming over me. Yet I could not turn my head to see who or what was there. At this point tears were streaming down my face, not as much from being frightened as from being completely frustrated at my inability to so much as wiggle my fingers. I tried everything I could, using reason to try and send the signals to my brain to move my body. After a bit of time—maybe ten or fifteen minutes, though I can't say for sure—I felt the presence withdraw. I heard footsteps move away from my bed toward the door, the sound of the door handle turn, the door open and close, and then the echo of the footsteps retreat back through the kitchen, down the hall, and out the front door of my apartment.

As soon as the front door closed, I was able to move. I jumped up, grabbed the key, and ran out of the bedroom. I could still hear the footsteps descending the inner stairwell, as I lunged toward the apartment door. I heard the outside door of the building slam shut, and I ran down the stairs and out the main door. I couldn't see anyone, so I ran down the path and looked right and left down the street. There was no one in sight. A fresh snow had fallen while I was asleep, and I could see no mark or footprint of where anyone had been on the path or the porch.

⊰ THE PALACE OF VERSAILLES ⊱

Just outside of Paris, France, among the rambling and vast grounds of the Palace of Versailles, stands Le Petit Trianon. Best known for being the residence of Marie Antoinette, Le Petit Trianon was given her name by King Louis XVI in 1774. Yet this mini palace within a palace is also famous for something else: hauntings.

Over the centuries guests and visitors have reported numerous sightings and unusual sounds. Most often workers in eighteenth-century clothing are seen milling about, and some people claim to have seen the ghost of Marie Antoinette herself. One of the strangest reports is of seeing phantom woodlands and houses that have not been there for more than two hundred years.

A FITFUL NIGHT IN BARCELONA
▶➤ AS TOLD BY K. R. P. ⟨◀

After weeks of traveling, I found myself in a small, dark room just off the main *La Rambla* in Barcelona, Spain. My girlfriend and I were very weary and grateful for the simple and affordable room. While my girlfriend slipped easily into a deep slumber, I tossed and turned, unable to fall asleep. I became keenly aware of a glowing sensation by and around the shuttered window. Irritated, I tried to ignore it, exhausted as I was. But I was unable to ignore it, and so I looked back toward the window. I clearly saw a man sitting with his back to me, at a desk in front of the window. (There was no actual desk in the room.) He appeared to be leaning forward, writing something down on paper. He took no notice of me whatsoever, and I felt no threat. I simply turned over and, at last, fell asleep.

⟨ THE HOLY GRAIL ⟩

This infamous object has been sought by scholars, scientists, and the devout for centuries. The Holy Grail is best known as the cup that Jesus used to drink from at the Last Supper, and that Jesus' uncle used to catch drops of Jesus' blood at the crucifixion. In order to escape persecution, the disciples of Jesus took the Grail to Glastonbury, England. There are countless legends surrounded the Grail and its mystical powers. Some believe it is a cauldron of magic, containing secrets of birth and death. Others argue that the Grail is not an object at all, but rather a state of spiritual enlightenment. Many chalices resting in museums around the world claim to be the actual Grail.

⟨ SACSAYHUAMAN ⟩

Locals help tourists remember the name of these ancient Inca ruins by laughingly telling them it is pronounced "sexy woman." On a hillside just above the town of Cuzco, Peru, the Sacsayhuaman ruins still bake in the golden light of the Inca's beloved sun. Most local history says that Cuzco was built in the shape of the sacred puma and Sacsayhuaman was the puma's head. The stone walls and monoliths of Sacsayhuaman were so expertly crafted that the Spanish conquistadores, convinced no mortal man could create stonework so perfect, thought the Sacsayhuaman must have been built by evil spirits.

⟨ A DAUGHTER'S LOVE ⟩

November of 1919 was an especially cold and difficult winter in the northern regions of Italy. Snow fell on Venice, and Dr. Antonio Salvatici was making his way down one of the canals in a covered gondola. The doctor was the bishop's personal physician and was leaving the church late after attending to an elderly member of the diocese.

From the banks of the canals, Dr. Salvatici heard the voice of a young girl crying for help. When the doctor looked through the falling snow to the street, he saw a little girl, clutching a shawl for warmth, calling to him. Her mother was ill, and the little girl was begging that he come tend to her.

Although he was surprised that the girl recognized him as a doctor, he nonetheless answered her plea and disembarked from the gondola, following the little girl to a court, then up a flight of stairs in one of the old houses. There he found a sick woman, who had a terrible case of pneumonia. As Salvatici attempted to ease the woman's pain, he said to her that she was lucky to have such a daughter, one who would brave the elements to come and find him to get her mother help.

At this the woman looked quite shocked, and reported to the doctor that her daughter had died one month before. Salvatici argued with her, telling the sick woman he had just seen her and followed her here. How else would he have known to go to her, just as she was at her sickest?

But the woman insisted her daughter had died and pointed to a cupboard where she kept her daughter's things. The doctor indulged the woman and opened the cabinet, only to discover the woman indeed had her young daughter's things—among them the very shawl, dry as a bone, that he had seen her clutching as she called to him in the snowy night. No trace of the little girl was found.

⟨ A MEMPHIS BELLE ⟩

The jewel of downtown Memphis, Tennessee, is the Orpheum Theater, a beautiful and ornate theater that hosts classic and modern acts ranging from musicals to Shakespeare to Tom Waits. The Orpheum has also been host to several supernatural events. Most common is the sighting of the ghost of a little girl. Many employees, docents, and historians agree that she is likely the spirit of a little girl who was killed around the turn of the twentieth century by a horse and carriage while crossing the street on her way to the theater. Other accounts say that a girl died when she fell from the upper balcony. While her cause of death is uncertain, there have been multiple sightings of the same little girl, who is known simply as Mary. She is spotted occasionally in the box seats and frequently in the theater before or after a concert or play.

⟨ THE SILVER QUEEN HOTEL ⟩

In Virginia City, Nevada, there is a hotel that has stood the test of time. First built in 1876, the Silver Queen Hotel still does not have phones, televisions, or alarm clocks in any of its twenty-nine rooms. Popular among history buffs and those who come to Virginia City to vacation and gamble, the Silver Queen has been host to countless wedding parties, anniversaries, and romance seekers. It also plays host to a few ghost hunters, for it is known for a high level of paranormal activity. While some people come specifically seeking ghosts, other, unsuspecting guests have been shocked to witness haunting activities.

One couple heard the sound of a banjo being tuned in the room next door, only to find the room empty when they went to investigate. The couple also heard an argument going on outside their door. When they flung open the door, they saw no one, but they still heard two voices arguing. The couple became convinced the hotel was haunted. They were later awakened by a loud pounding at their door, but when they answered, they found only the empty hall.

Other guests have reported hearing creaks, footsteps, and doors opening and closing.

⟨ TO MARKET, TO MARKET ⟩

Pike Place Market in Seattle, Washington, is a well-known attraction in the city's bustling downtown. Apart from a rich history and stalls overflowing with wares, the Market is also home to several legendary ghosts—an elderly Native American woman, a little boy, a large woman, and a tall African-American man. Shopkeepers and tourists alike have reported strange goings-on throughout the years, including sightings of these spirits, footsteps in empty aisles, and items out of place.

⟨ ORIGINS OF THE OUIJA ⟩

The Ouija is any surface printed with letters, numbers, and other symbols and used as a tool to communicate with the dead. The Ouija Board, which was patented by the Parker Brothers in 1920, is what most commonly comes to mind when thinking of the Ouija. The word "ouija" is believed to stem from "oui," meaning "yes" in French, and "ja" meaning "yes" in Scandinavian languages and in German. Other stories say that the name of the tool was revealed to inventor Charles Kennard during a séance and that "ouija" is actually an Ancient Egyptian word meaning "good luck."

Dominoes originated in Asia around A.D. 1100. They were, and still are, used as a divinatory tool and not just a game of numbers.

A WEDDING NIGHT VISITOR
►⊱ AS TOLD BY K. R. P. ⊰◄

It was the night before my fiancée and I were to be wed. We had chosen a beautiful B&B, the Willard Street Inn, in Burlington, Vermont, for lodging and holding the intimate ceremony. Upon arrival, we were given the run of the place and told we could choose any room we wanted. My wife-to-be and I chose the Tower Room, primarily for its view of Lake Champlain.

I slept fitfully, tossing and turning until I fell into an exhausted slumber. I hadn't been asleep long when I awoke quite suddenly and sat up. In front of me was a man in his fifties, wearing a tuxedo. He appeared to be trying to make a bed that would have been perpendicular to the bed we were in. He took no notice of me but continued with what seemed to be his normal rounds. I did not feel any threat, and, quite tired, I rolled over and went back to sleep.

2. THE ANNUAL CHICKEN SHOW

ENCHANTED ANIMALS, PSYCHIC PETS, BOTANICAL ODDITIES, AND OTHER STRANGE TRUTHS ABOUT MOTHER NATURE

⊰ THE ANNUAL CHICKEN SHOW ⊱

Held the second Saturday in July in Wayne, Nebraska, the Annual Chicken Show features a crowing contest for roosters, a free omelet feed for humans, and a chicken-flying meet, fully sanctioned by the International Chicken Flying Association. Included events are a "Most Beautiful Beak" contest, chicken bingo, and an egg drop (participants risk getting egg on their faces by trying to catch a raw egg dropped from a fully extended cherry picker). The National Cluck-Off selects the person with the most lifelike cluck and most believable crow. Another contest offers prizes to the man and woman who sport the most chickenlike legs.

According to *National Wildlife Magazine*, dolphins experience unihemispheric sleep: one half of the brain rests while the other half stays vigilantly awake. Dolphins sleep with one eye closed—the eye opposite the dozing half of the brain.

⟨ MIKE, THE HEADLESS WONDER CHICKEN ⟩

In 1945, farmer Lloyd Olsen of Fruita, Colorado, went to his barnyard to butcher a chicken for his family's dinner. But the chicken in question had other ideas.

Olsen skillfully beheaded the fowl with a swift ax chop, and the body, like those of so many freshly killed chickens, began to stagger around. Then it took off running. The next day, Olsen found the headless rooster, still alive and pecking. Unable to kill a bird with such a clear will to live, the farmer began using an eyedropper to feed grain and water down its esophagus. He then drove the bird 250 miles to the University of Utah in Salt Lake City. There, scientists determined that Olsen's ax blow had missed the rooster's jugular vein, and a subsequent blood clot had kept the bird from bleeding to death. The brain stem, which controlled most of the bird's reflexive functions, remained attached to the body. Oblivious to the fact that most of his head was missing, the rooster continued trying to peck for food, preening its feathers, and sleeping with the top of his neck under his wing.

Over the next eighteen months, Olsen continued to use an eyedropper to feed the bird, who flourished in spite of his handicap, growing from two and a half pounds to a robust eighteen pounds. Dubbed Mike, the

Headless Wonder Chicken, the plucky rooster and Olsen set off on a national tour and became the subject of articles in *Time* and *Life* magazines. Unfortunately, Mike's miraculous life came to an abrupt end in an Arizona hotel. The rooster choked, and Olsen was unable to find an eyedropper to clear his feathered friend's throat.

Today, Mike still has his own fan club, and his dauntless spirit is celebrated annually in Fruita on the third weekend in May. "Mike's Festival" includes a chicken-recipe contest, a chicken-dance contest, and a 5K "run like a headless chicken." Appropriately, the event's Web site states, "Attending this fun, family event is a no-brainer."

⟨ ANIMAL CRIMINALS ⟩

Centuries ago, animals were often put on trial for crimes ranging from witchcraft to theft to murder.

Throughout history, the animal that's been prosecuted most in court is the pig. In 1547 France, for example, a mother pig and her six babies were sentenced to death for killing and eating a child. The sow was executed, but the piglets were pardoned because it was felt that they were led astray by the bad example of their mother.

The only known criminal hanging of an elephant took place in Erwin, Tennessee, on September 13, 1916. The convict's name was Five-Ton Mary, and she had killed a keeper.

In 1963, the courts of Tripoli sentenced seventy-five convicted banknote smugglers to death at one time. They were all pigeons.

⊰ EARLIEST DOCTORS ⊱

Chimpanzees exhibit an apparent knowledge and use of medicinal plants. They have been recorded using thirteen different plant genera from eight families as medications for a variety of ailments. Indigenous populations of the same regions use many of the same plants to treat a variety of stomach upsets, headaches, and parasitic infections. Chimpanzees seem to have an extensive knowledge of which part of the plant to use; they have been seen consuming the leaves, the pith, and the roots during times of illness.

⊰ NOT CUTE ⊱

According to the book *Weird U.S.*, more than one person reported spotting a humungous penguin waddling down Clearwater Beach, Florida, in 1998. The bird was reportedly a striking fifteen feet tall and left giant web tracks in the sand. Around the same time, boaters in the gulf told reporters about a huge penguinlike bird they'd seen floating in the water, and a pilot claimed to have seen a creature of a similar description on the banks of the Suwannee River.

"The phoenix hope, can wing her way through the desert skies, and still defying fortune's spite; revive from ashes and rise." —MIGUEL DE CERVANTES

⤙ THE FOURTEEN-TOED TAPIR ⤚

Baird's tapir is the largest land mammal in Central America, with a range from southern Mexico to northwestern Colombia. Tapirs are elusive and agile animals who move expertly through vast and varied terrain—from steep slopes to rivers. Uniquely, they have four front toes but only three back ones, for a total of fourteen toes.

⤙ PUTS NESSIE TO SHAME ⤚

Everyone knows about the legend of the Loch Ness Monster, the huge, snakelike creature that supposedly terrorizes a lake in Scotland. Fewer have heard about Caddy of Puget Sound, Washington. Caddy sports a long neck and a shrunken, horselike head, and is estimated to be at least forty feet long.

Lake Memphremagog, on the international border between Vermont and Quebec, boasts its own sea monster, nicknamed Memphré. Sightings of the huge, serpentlike creature date back to the early nineteenth century and have continued into the twenty-first century.

⤙ FORTEAN FROGS ⤚

Though typically a biblical phenomenon, raining animals have been reported around the world. The two most common of these animals are fish and frogs; however, there have even been accounts of falling jellyfish, worms, and ducks. Charles Fort, a nineteenth-century writer and researcher of strange phenomena, included "true" stories about falling frogs in his *Book of the Damned*.

CURIOUS CATS

►> MAGICAL CAT <◄

King Charles I of England (1600–1649) got the idea that if he lost his beloved black cat, it would mean a disaster for him, so he had the animal guarded constantly. Unfortunately, the cat got sick and died. Strangely enough, Charles was right—the day after the cat died, he was arrested for treason and, not long afterward, beheaded.

►> FELINE FEARS <◄

U.S. Attorney General John Ashcroft suffers from aelurophobia (or ailurophobia)—a deathly fear of cats. He is afraid of calicos in particular.

►> CATS LOVE HEART <◄

When English writer Thomas Hardy (1840–1928) died, his heart was kept apart when his body was cremated. The idea was to bury it in Stinsford, England, the home of his beloved childhood church and his family's burial plot. All went according to plan until his sister's cat leaped up onto her kitchen table, snatched the heart, and ran off into the woods with it.

►►‣ THAT'S A LOT OF KITTY LITTER ‣◄◄

The record for ownership of the most cats goes to Jack and Donna Wright of Kingston, Ontario, according to the *Guinness Book of World Records*. The couple owns a staggering 689 felines, many descended from the cat that started it all: a tabby called Midnight, whom Donna picked up in 1970.

►►‣ LIFE SAVER ‣◄◄

A couple named Irma and Gianni lived in a village near Mount Vesuvius in the 1940s. One evening in 1944, their cat became agitated and tried to get the couple out of bed by jumping on them, scratching, and eventually chasing Gianni around the room. Gianni was enraged and wanted to throw the cat outside. Irma, however, felt that the cat was trying to tell them to leave. She insisted that they pack some clothes and get out. Soon after, Vesuvius erupted, covering their village in lava and killing many people. Irma and Gianni's cat had saved them from that fate.

►►‣ CRUEL AND UNUSUAL PUNISHMENT ‣◄◄

As recently as the late nineteenth century, women accused of adultery in Turkey were tied in bags with live cats and thrown into the ocean.

⊰ IS FIDO PSYCHIC? ⊱

Many people claim their pets have extrasensory perception (ESP), and a Russian experiment proved it. To test dogs' mind-reading abilities, the scientists conducted 1,278 trials that measured the canine's response to unspoken commands. The dogs responded correctly to the unspoken commands more than 50 percent of the time. The odds of this phenomenon being mere chance, claims Dennis Bardens, the author of *Psychic Animals*, are billions to one.

THE ANNUAL FIRE ANT FESTIVAL: ⊰ A WEIRD CELEBRATION ⊱

In South Texas, the fire ant (red ants that swarm and bite) is a real problem. But in Marshall, Texas, the people decided that since they couldn't get rid of these pests, they might as well have some fun with them. So they started the annual Fire Ant Festival. Special events include the fire ant call, fire ant roundup, and a fire ant chili cookoff in which entrants must certify in writing that their ingredients include at least one fire ant. The ending to the festivities is the Fire Ant Stomp, which is not an attempt to squash the ants, but an old-fashioned street dance.

"Therefore I will wail and howl, I will go stripped and naked: I will make a wailing like the dragons, and mourning as the owls." —MICAH 1:8

ENTHRALLING ARACHNIDS

▶▶ MAGICAL SPIDER WEBS ◀◀

› Only about half of all spider species spin webs to catch their prey.

› All spider webs are made of silk. Although it's only about 0.00012 inch in diameter, a spider's silk is stronger than steel of equal diameter. It is more elastic than nylon, more difficult to break than rubber, and is bacteria and fungi resistant. These qualities explain why at one time webs were used to pack wounds to help them stop bleeding.

› Spiders have one to six kinds of spinning glands, each producing a different type of silk. For instance, the cylindrical gland produces silk used for egg sacs (males often lack this particular gland), and the aciniform gland produces silk used for wrapping prey. Some spiders have glands that produce very fine silk. They comb and tease the fine strands until they are like Velcro—tiny loops and hooks that entrap insect feet.

➤ Silk is extruded through special pores called spinneretes, which consist of different-sized "spigots." Silk starts out as a liquid. As the liquid silk contacts the air, it hardens. The spider may need different silk for different purposes. By changing how fast the liquid is extruded or by using a different silk gland, it can control the strength and quality of the silk.

➤ Why doesn't a spider get stuck on its own web? The spider weaves in nonsticky silk strands and only walks on those. Also, spiders have special oil on their legs that keeps them from sticking to the silk.

➤➤ THE WELL-BRED SPIDER ◄◄

A spider can often be identified by the type of web it weaves. The ability to weave is inherited, so specific types of spiders build specific types of webs. In addition, individual spiders sometimes develop a personal style, sort of like a signature.

The spider is a hunter, and its web is a snare designed to hold its prey. So the design of its web and the place where the spider builds it depend on the kind of insects it is trying to catch. There are more insects, especially crawling ones, closer to the ground. Spiders often spin webs across ground litter such as leaves and fallen branches where an unsuspecting insect may crawl. Strong flying insects are usually higher, so webs built high are stronger than those built in low spots.

 WEB SPINNERS

There are five different types of web-spinning spiders. One kind is cobweb spiders, such as black widows. They use their webs as "trip lines" to snare prey. From their web, several vertical lines are drawn down and secured tautly to a surface with globs of "glue." Insects get stuck to the glue and break the line. The tension of the elastic trip lines, once released, flings the victim up to the spider waiting in its web. Cobweb weavers usually build only one web and so, with time, the web becomes tattered and littered with bits of debris.

The second kind of web spinner is called a sheet-builder. They construct a horizontal mat beneath a horizontal trip line, much like a trampoline under an invisible wire. Flying or jumping insects that are stopped midair by the line are flung to the net below, and as the prey struggles to regain its balance, the agile spider pounces and inflicts a deadly bite.

Web-casting spiders, such as ogre-faced spiders, are the third kind of web spinner. They use "web snares" much differently than others. Instead of attaching the web to a bush or a wall, the spider carries it. The spider uses the web much like a fishing net and casts it on passing prey. The spider hunts every night and afterward will either tuck the web away until the next day's hunt or spin a new one.

Then there are the angle lines, such as the bola spider. It first suspends itself from a trapeze line and hangs there upside down. Then it sends down a single line baited with a glob of glue. When an insect moves by, the bola takes careful aim and casts the line toward the insect. If successful, it will reel in its prize easily.

Lastly, there are orb weavers. These weavers spin the largest and strongest webs. Some webs span more than one meter. Natives of New Guinea and the Solomon Islands used the webs of the orb-weaving spiders as fishing nets. These webs were reportedly strong enough to hold a fish weighing as much as a pound. These webs are especially tailored to capture flying insects, which is why they're vertically suspended. Many orb weavers meticulously take down their webs each day and build a new one at night.

Orb weavers spin such intricate webs that they are often the focus of behavioral studies. For example, two orb weavers went along on Sky Lab II on July 28, 1973.

Researchers were interested to know the effects of zero gravity on the spiders' weaving ability. After some adjustments, the spiders were able to weave fairly normal webs. One curious difference was that the space webs were symmetrical, while earth webs tend to be asymmetrical.

RECLUSIVE STILL

Only eight hundred deaths from brown recluse spiders have been verified in medical literature since 1965, but more than eight hundred death certificates list a cause of death as "hemolytic anemia," an allergic reaction to—the bite of the brown recluse.

⟨ TRUE SLOTH ⟩

In 2007, after three years of failed attempts to entice a sloth into budging as part of an experiment in animal movement, scientists in the eastern German city of Jena gave up. The sloth, named Mats, was remanded to a zoo after consistently refusing to climb up and then back down a pole as part of an experiment conducted by scientists at the University of Jena's Institute of Systematic Zoology and Evolutionary Biology.

Neither pounds of cucumbers nor plates of home-made spaghetti were appetizing enough to make Mats move. Mats's new home is the zoo in the northwestern city of Duisburg where, according to all reports, he is very comfortable.

※※※※※※※※※※※※※※※※※※※※※※※※※※※※※※※※※※

➤ A rat can last longer without water than a camel. Rats can also hold their breath for three minutes and tread water for three days.
➤ Rats multiply so quickly that in eighteen months, two rats could have over a million descendants.

※※※※※※※※※※※※※※※※※※※※※※※※※※※※※※※※※※

⟨ THE RAT TALES ⟩

Deserved or not, rats have always received bad press. One reason the Egyptians had a cat goddess was because her feline children ate the rodents that ate Egyptian grain. We remember Dick Whittington and his cat, because the cat saved London from an invasion of rats—rats carrying the Black Death—in the Middle Ages.

There is only one known rat goddess. The Male-kulans, who live on the island of Vanuatu in the South Pacific, have a goddess named Le-Hev-Hev, whose name translates as "she who smiles so we can draw near and she can eat us." They offered her boars so she wouldn't eat human corpses.

The best rat story concerns the Pied Piper, that magical fellow who lived in early thirteenth-century Germany and had a magic flute whose tune attracted rats. He traveled about the countryside offering to drive the rats out of towns and into a cave under a mountain for a fee. When he visited Hamelin, the good burghers hired him, and he whistled the rats away. But the burghers neglected to pay him. So the Pied Piper changed his tune and led the town's children under the mountain with his whistle.

▶❯ WHEN RATS TAKE OVER ❰◀

During the Middle Ages, the Catholic Church decided that cats were agents of the devil and ordered the extermination of all felines. For two hundred years, there were cat burnings and other forms of cat murder. If you tried to protect your puss, you could be burned at the stake as a witch. Consequently, the population of cats in Europe was decimated, which had an effect the church hadn't considered—the rat population, now unchecked, exploded. And so did the Black Plague, which was spread by fleas on rats. By the time the church saw the error of its ways and reversed its order, decreeing that good Christians must treat cats kindly, 75 percent of the population of Europe had died in the Plague. Cats' revenge, perhaps?

⟨ A WHALE OF A TIME ⟩

Female blue whales give birth to calves every two to three years. Pregnancy lasts for about one year. A newborn calf is about 23 feet (7 m) long and weighs 5,000 to 6,000 pounds (2,700 kg). A nursing mother produces over 50 gallons (200 liters) of milk a day. The milk contains 35 to 50 percent fat and allows the calf to gain weight at a rate of up to 10 pounds an hour—or over 250 pounds (44 kg) a day! At six months the calf is weaned, and at that point its average length is about 52 feet (16 m). The blue whale reaches sexual maturity in ten years.

⟨ WOMAN'S BEST FRIEND ⟩

A woman in California who ran a successful coffee business had her canine companion constantly at her side. One afternoon while taking a much needed break, her dear doggie began to sniff and lick at her breast area. That night, her dog repeated the odd behavior by tugging at the blankets and biting at her pajama shirt. The next day, the canine jumped into her lap and dove at her breasts, which caused some pain. She was stunned to discover that she had a lump in her breast, and later medical tests revealed it to be a cancerous tumor. She had had a routine breast exam just three months earlier, but the odd behavior of her dog saved her life. If the tumor had developed more extensively, it could have spread into her lymph nodes. After months of chemotherapy and radiation, she is now living cancer free.

> OAK TREES DO NOT PRODUCE ACORNS UNTIL THEY ARE AT LEAST FIFTY YEARS OLD.

⟨ FIBONACCI FLOWERS ⟩

Plants with spiral patterns related to the golden angle (an angle related to the golden ration or "divine proportion") consistently display another fascinating mathematical property: the seeds of the flower head form interlocking spirals going both clockwise and counterclockwise. These numbers of seeds are almost always two consecutive Fibonacci numbers. Fibonacci numbers form a sequence in which each number is the sum of the previous two (1, 1, 2, 3, 5, 8, 13, and so on).

➤ *Daphnomancy* is the word for divination through bay leaves. The word pays homage to Daphne, a nymph from ancient Greek myths who was turned into the first bay laurel tree when fleeing Apollo's flirtatious advances.

➤ The eggplant is a member of the thistle family.

➤ Throughout the 1500s to the 1700s, tobacco was prescribed as medicine for a variety of complaints, including headaches, toothaches, arthritis, and bad breath.

‹ HEROIC HERBAL ›

Yarrow, *Alchillea millefolium*, takes its Latin name from Achilles, the invincible Greek warrior who had but one vulnerable spot—his heel. When his heel was sliced, yarrow was used to assuage the bleeding. Even today, one of the most well-known medicinal uses for yarrow is to staunch bleeding. The shape of the yarrow's leaves also form tiny arrows, which look like Achilles's bow and arrow. Yarrow was also used as the original sticks in the Chinese oracle, the I-Ching.

MORBID PLANTS

►►❯ VAMPIRE LILY (*DRACUNCULUS VULGARIS*) ❮◄◄

No freakish garden is complete without the beloved vampire lily, *Dracunculus vulgaris*. Also called the dragon arum, it belongs to the *Araceae* family. Sporting an incredible, deep red flower with a ruffled edge and a long black or deep purple spadix, the vampire lily brings to mind the gown you wished you had for last Halloween's costume contest. Even the stems are gothic looking; they are a mottled green and red, as if they have been splattered with blood. One of the creepiest aspects of this plant, and no doubt what brought on the fantastically vampiric associations, is the fact that it emits a smell like that of rotting flesh. This scent attracts the flies and carrion beetles that pollinate it. The flower's deceptive beauty lures human garden visitors into its realm, enticing them to put their noses into the blood red curls of the blossom and inhale deeply, only to be horrified and repelled by the flower's sweet and sickening smell of death.

What could be more bewitching than a plant with such a ghoulish name? The voodoo lily, *Sauromatum guttatum*, sometimes identified as *S. venosum*, derives its name from its speckled, bloody red flower foul, corpse-like smell. Adapted to attract flies and beetles as its pollinators, the voodoo lily's flower forms with a tall central spike, or spadix, surrounded by the spathe. For the voodoo lily, the spadix is the richest of reds, and the spathe is a vibrant red spotted with deep burgundy. Especially enchanting even when not in bloom, the voodoo lily has speckled leaf spikes that appear after the single flower has come and gone, shooting up and branching out to look like miniature gothic tropical trees, green and smattered with blood red spots at the base. The voodoo lily is bizarre, enchanting, and gorgeously ghastly.

►▶ THE CORPSE FLOWER (*AMORPHOPHALLUS TITANUM*) ◀◄

No list of botanical oddities would be complete without the one and only corpse flower. Named for its extremely potent, corpselike smell, *Amorphophallus titanum* is also one of the largest flower structures in the world. Growing up to twelve feet tall and five feet wide in the wild, with leaves that can exceed twenty feet, the corpse flower, also known as the titan arum, is both ghastly and breathtaking. (You actually will want to hold your breath when near it in its fullest bloom.) The flower comes before the leaves, although the plant needs to be at least six years old before it can bloom. When it does, a large mottled spike pushes up from the ground, slowly unfurling to reveal a beautiful, deep red, velvet outer spathe and a three-foot, dirty green spike in the center. When fully opened, the bloom of the corpse flower begins to live up to its rotten reputation, for it emits the strongest and most foul of decomposing fleshlike odors. The smell is caused by the most wicked of essential oils—putrecines and cadavarines.

A foul beauty, the corpse flower looks like something from the musical *Little Shop of Horrors*, and anyone who has seen and smelled it will not quickly forget its cadaverous horrors.

▶▷ OTHER FREAKY, STINKY PLANTS ◁◀

There are, besides the vampire lily, the voodoo lily, and the corpse flower, many other unusual plants in the *Araceae* family. For blood red and blackish flowers, check out *Arum apulum*, *A. dioscoridis*, *A. oriental*, and *A. pictum*, as well as *Biarum tenufolium* and *Biarum tenufolium* var. *zeleborii*. Another plant that smells of rotting flesh is the aptly named dead horse arum, *Helicodiceros muschivorus*.

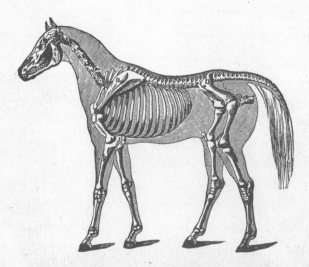

THE BOOK OF THE BIZARRE

3. HISTORY'S MYSTERIES

BIZARRE BUT TRUE FACTS ABOUT HISTORICAL FIGURES,
AND ODDITIES FROM TODAY AND YESTERDAY

FAMOUS NAMES, UNFORTUNATE DEATHS

▶❯ BENJAMIN FRANKLIN'S DEATH ❮◀

Benjamin Franklin died, strangely enough, from complications from sitting in front of an open window. Franklin was a big believer in fresh air, even in the middle of winter. He slept with the windows open year-round, and, as he wrote, "I rise almost every morning and sit in my chamber without any clothes whatever, half an hour or an hour, according to the season." In April 1790, the eighty-four-year-old Franklin developed an abscess in his lungs, which his doctor blamed on too many hours spent sitting at the open window. The abscess burst on April 17, sending him into a coma. He died a few hours later.

▶❯ THE DEATH OF JOSEPH STALIN ❮◀

Soviet dictator Joseph Stalin, who murdered millions of his own country's people, may have been the last victim of his own reign of terror. On the evening of March 1, 1953, the seventy-four-year-old Stalin stayed up drinking with his cronies until 4 A.M. His normal habit was to rise again around noon, but that day he didn't.

As the hours passed and Stalin did not emerge from his private quarters, his aides began to panic. They didn't want to risk his wrath, but they were worried. At 10:30 P.M., they finally worked up the nerve to enter his apartments, where they found him sprawled out on his living room floor, paralyzed by a stroke, and unable to speak. The terrified aides still did not know what to do, so they didn't call for the Kremlin doctors until 8:30 the following morning! By then it was too late: according to Stalin's daughter Svetlana, the dictator died a difficult and terrible death four days later.

━━▶❯ THE EUTHANIZATION OF KING GEORGE V ❮◀━━

King George V of England, grandfather of Queen Elizabeth II, was euthanized with morphine and cocaine to meet a newspaper deadline.

The king, a heavy smoker, was in the final stages of lung disease on January 20, 1936. His death was imminent. The date of the state funeral had been set, and the London *Times* had been instructed to hold the presses—a death announcement would be coming soon. But that night, as the newspaper's deadline loomed, the king still held on. The king's doctor, who saw that the king's condition might last for many more hours and disrupt the arrangements, decided to euthanize him so that the morning papers could still make the announcement that the king was dead.

▶▶ DIAMOND JIM BRADY ◀◀

Turn-of-the-twentieth-century millionaire, collector of fine gems (hence the nickname), and one of the world's all-time great eaters, Diamond Jim Brady, in fact, ate himself to death.

A typical day for Brady started with a breakfast of steak, eggs, cornbread, muffins, pancakes, pork chops, fried potatoes, and hominy, washed down with a gallon or more of orange juice. Breakfast was followed with snacks at 11:30, lunch at 12:30, and afternoon tea—all of which involved enormous quantities of food. Dinner often consisted of three dozen oysters, six crabs, two bowls of soup, seven lobsters, two ducks, two servings of turtle meat, plus steak, vegetables, a full platter of pastries, and a two-pound box of chocolates.

When Brady suffered an attack of gallstones in 1912, his surgeons opened him up and found that his stomach was *six* times the normal size of a human stomach and covered in so many layers of fat they couldn't complete the surgery. Diamond Jim ignored their advice to cut back, yet hung on another five years, albeit in considerable pain from diabetes, bad kidneys, stomach ulcers, and heart problems. He died of a heart attack in 1917.

CATHERINE THE GREAT

There are probably more rumors about the death of Catherine the Great, the empress of Russia, than that of any other monarch in history. Most of them relate to her reputedly unusual sexual appetites. For some reason, many people believe a horse was being lowered onto her when the cable holding the horse aloft snapped, crushing her. That is a complete myth—perhaps invented by the French, Russia's enemies at the time.

What really happened? Two weeks after suffering a mild stroke at the age of sixty-seven, Catherine appeared to be recovering. On November 5, she began her day with her usual routine, rising at 8 A.M., drinking several cups of coffee, and going to spend ten minutes in the bathroom. But she did not come out after ten minutes, and when her footman finally looked in on her, he found her sprawled out on the floor, bleeding and barely alive. Like Elvis Presley, she had a stroke while sitting on the toilet. She died the next day.

▬ ▸▸❯ GEORGE EASTMAN ❮◂◂ ▬

George Eastman, the founder of Eastman Kodak and the father of modern photography, committed suicide. In 1932, Eastman was seventy-eight years old and felt tired and ill. On March 14, he updated his will, and later in the day, he asked his doctor and his nurses to leave the room, telling them he wanted to write a note. It turned out to be a suicide note. He wrote the note, put out his cigarette, removed his glasses, and shot himself in the heart.

▬ ▸▸❯ ISADORA DUNCAN ❮◂◂ ▬

Isadora Duncan, one of the world's most famous dancers, died from a broken neck. On September 14, 1927, Duncan climbed into the passenger seat of a Bugatti race car wearing a long red silk scarf. The scarf was a little too long: when the car started off, the tail end wrapped around the wheel and yanked Duncan out of the car, snapping her neck and dragging her for several yards before the driver realized what had happened. In an eerie twist, the day before she died, Duncan had told an *Associated Press* reporter, "I'm frightened that some quirk accident may happen."

➤ MARGARET MITCHELL ◄

Margaret Mitchell, the author of *Gone with the Wind*, was run down by an automobile when she was crossing busy Peachtree Street in downtown Atlanta with her husband. She was halfway across when she saw a speeding motorist bearing down on her. Mitchell had previously said she was certain she would die in a car crash. Perhaps that's why she panicked, darting back across the street and leaving her husband standing in the middle of the road. She got hit; he did not. She died in the hospital five days later. The driver who hit her turned out to be a twenty-nine-year-old taxi driver with twenty-three traffic violations on his record.

➤ NELSON ROCKEFELLER ◄

When Nelson Rockefeller, the former governor of New York, the vice president under Gerald Ford, the grandson of John D. Rockefeller, and founder of Standard Oil, died in 1979 at age seventy-one, official reports said he had a heart attack while sitting at his desk. Later, this story was found to be a cover-up. He was actually alone in his townhouse with twenty-five-year-old Megan Marshack, who was on Rockefeller's staff. She supposedly had been working with him on a book about his modern-art collection, but, as the

New York *Daily News* reported, there were no work papers at his house—just food and wine. So how did he really die? What really happened? Two people know, and one of them died.

OFF WITH HER HEAD

The execution of Mary, Queen of Scots, was not the somber operation it should have been. The executioner was not used to executing women, and he was nervous. The first blow missed Mary's neck entirely, hitting the back of her head instead. The second and third attempts hit their target, but didn't cut the queen's neck completely. When the execution was finally complete, the executioner tried to hold up the severed head to show the audience, as was the custom. But he failed to notice that the queen had been wearing a wig, and the head slipped from his hand and bounced three times on the ground.

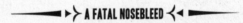

A FATAL NOSEBLEED

Attila the Hun did not die in battle, as many believe. He met his maker on his wedding night. After a night of lovemaking, he got a nasty nosebleed and lost so much blood that he died.

⟨ NAPOLEON'S CODE ⟩

Napoleon Bonaparte used an oracular system based on a series of random dots. This system is a version of what is commonly known as geomancy, but which has come to be referred to as the *Oracle de Napoleon*. While not a great deal is known about the actual details of the system (Napoleon kept them a closely guarded secret), several attempts have been made to reconstruct it. None are proven to be the exact system he used, although there are versions that have been "confirmed" by a woman who claims to have traveled throughout France with Napoleon's company and witnessed his use of the system on several occasions. She revealed the system after his death.

⟨ WHAT GOES AROUND COMES AROUND ⟩

Fleming was a poor Scottish farmer. One day, while trying to make a living for his family, he heard a cry for help coming from a nearby bog. He dropped his tools and ran to the bog. There, mired to his waist in black muck, was a terrified boy, screaming and struggling to free himself. Farmer Fleming saved the lad from what could have been a slow and terrifying death.

The next day, a fancy carriage pulled up to the Scotsman's sparse surroundings. An elegantly dressed nobleman stepped out and introduced himself as the father of the boy Farmer Fleming had saved. The nobleman offered to repay Farmer Fleming for saving his son's life, but the farmer would not accept payment. At that moment, Farmer Fleming's own son came to the door of the family hovel. The nobleman and the farmer struck up a deal that he would provide Farmer Fleming's son with the same level of education that his son would enjoy. His son attended the very best schools, and in time, graduated from St. Mary's Hospital Medical School in London. He went on to become known throughout the world as the noted Sir Alexander Fleming, the discoverer of penicillin.

Years afterward, the same nobleman's son who was saved from the bog was stricken with pneumonia. What saved his life this time? Penicillin. The name of the nobleman? Lord Randolph Churchill. His son's name? Sir Winston Churchill.

⟨ THE UGLY PICKUP PARADE AND CONTEST ⟩

In 1987, newspaper columnist Les Mann wrote an homage to his junker 1974 pickup, "Black Beauty," claiming it was the ugliest truck on the planet. Irate ugly-truck owners wrote in, saying they could top him. And so the first Ugly Truck Contest was born, in Chadron, Nebraska. Experts pick the Ugly Pickup of the Year. The official rules are that trucks have to be street legal and over a decade old. They have to be able to move under their own power, a majority of their surface area has to be rust and dents, and, most importantly, they've got to have a good Ugly Truck name. Contestants get extra points for something especially ugly about their truck.

⟨ MARY KING'S CLOSE ⟩

The macabre past of Mary King's Close, located in the Old Town section of Edinburgh, Scotland, and sealed off in the 1600s, is seeing the light of day again. In 2003 the close was reopened, becoming a new tourist attraction—a preserved slice of seventeenth-century life.

Much mystery surrounds Mary King's Close. For centuries, locals have told tales of the close being sealed off to prevent the spread of the Plague. No evidence disputes this story, and there are some who say that the quarantine was voluntary. But lifelong inhabitants of Edinburgh say that after the close was sealed off, those outside heard anguished cries of people dying of starvation and begging to be let out. And they say that after the close was reopened, finger marks were found clawed into the bricks.

Mary King's Close is now open to the public and is the site of much paranormal and historical investigation. It is thought to be one of the most haunted places in Scotland.

⟨ SCRYING FOR LAMAS ⟩

Every Tibetan Dalai Lama is the reincarnation of his predecessor. After the thirteenth Dalai Lama died in 1933, the search for his replacement began. Lake Lhamoi Latso at Chokhorgyal, Tibet, is a lake long believed by Tibetans to reveal visions of the future. So the regent of the government-appointed search party traveled to Lake Lahmoi Latso, hoping that meditation and prayer would help him find the next Dalai Lama. After several days the regent saw a vision in the lake waters: a great monastery with green and gold roofs, and near the monastery, a small building with turquoise tiles. The young boy who was destined to be the fourteenth Dalai Lama lived in a house with turquoise tiles.

⟨ NO FEAR ⟩

The first human cannonball was a beautiful young girl named Zazel. She was only fourteen when the London circus she worked for recruited her for the honor. Zazel was catapulted out of the cannon not with gunpowder, as is widely believed, but with elastic springs that made no sound; the circus used firecrackers to create sparks and crackling sounds that mimicked gunpowder.

"In modern America, anyone who attempts to write satirically about the events of the day finds it difficult to concoct a situation so bizarre that it may not actually come to pass while the article is still on the presses." —CALVIN TRILLIN

⟨ ARMAGEDDON BRAS ⟩

In 1999, the *Times* of London reported that the firm Triumph International Japan had invented a bra that lets its wearer know of any incoming missiles. Called the Armageddon bra, it was designed to take advantage of the doomsday-prophecy craze sweeping Japan. It had a sensor on the strap and a control box. Unfortunately, it didn't work all that well under clothes; to be most effective, it had to be worn on the outside. No word on how many women took advantage of this spin on bust control.

⟨ BATHING BEAUTIES ⟩

Cleopatra is said to have bathed in donkey milk, and Mary Queen of Scots bathed in wine. Novelist George Sands preferred cow's milk (three quarts) and honey (three pounds). Isabeau, queen of France in the late twelfth century, was renowned for her beauty. To keep her looks, she used a beauty regimen that included bathing in asses' milk and rubbing crocodile glands and the brains of boars onto her skin.

⟨ PAIN FOR BEAUTY ⟩

For thousands of years, women poisoned themselves with their face makeup by using ceruse, a powder that caused lead poisoning. Rouge, too, was not safe—it contained mercury, which leads to miscarriages and birth defects.

- Chicago's Lincoln Park, created in 1864, was originally a burial ground. The 120-acre cemetery had most of its graves removed and was expanded to more than 1,000 acres for recreational use.
- The first city in the U.S. to fluoridate its water was Grand Rapids, Michigan, in 1945.
- The first state to use the gas chamber was Nevada in 1924.
- The Declaration of Independence was signed on July 4, 1776, but only by Charles Thomson and John Hancock. The majority of the people signed it on August 2, and the final signature wasn't until five years later.

⟨ EDISON'S PARANORMAL EXPERIMENTS ⟩

Thomas Edison was a scientist and legendary inventor, but he also held great interest in the paranormal. In 1948 the Philosophical Library published a book called *The Diary and Sundry Observations of Thomas Alva Edison*, which is a collection of Edison's personal essays, letters, and journal entries. Much of the content talks about his attempts to communicate with the beyond and his numerous experiments contacting the dead and the afterlife.

 ## ⟨ THE NUN CAME BACK ⟩

A young Bernadette Soubirous saw the Virgin Mary at a cave near Lourdes, France, at the tender age of fourteen. When she told people of what she'd seen, she was accused of lying, but within two weeks water began to trickle from the same cave, and it became renowned as a place of healing. Bernadette was declared a visionary and a saint.

Ironically, Bernadette herself never benefited from the healing waters, suffering a variety of ailments, including asthma and tuberculosis. The Sisters of Nevers, the local convent, cared for Bernadette until her death at the age of thirty-five, in the year 1879.

A few decades after someone believed to be a saint has died, it is customary to dig up his or her body to see if it remained intact. Bernadette's body did, in fact, remain quite preserved. Her recovered body was washed and then reinterred. Several years later, in 1919, she was again dug up and again found in a preserved state. She was reburied, only to be dug up once more in 1925, forty-six years after her death. Her body was remarkably well preserved, so much so that she was put on display at the Church of St. Gildard in Nevers, where she sits to this day.

Seventeenth-century queen Anne of England gave birth to seventeen children. Of these, only one made it past infancy, and even then the child lived until only the age of twelve.

⟨ SEVEN WONDERS OF THE ANCIENT WORLD ⟩

Can you name them?
- Pyramids at Giza
- Statue of Zeus at Olympia
- Hanging gardens of Babylon
- Colossus of Rhodes
- Lighthouse at Alexandria
- Temple of Artemis at Ephesus
- Mausoleum at Halicarnassus

> "HISTORY COULD PASS FOR A SCARLET TEXT, ITS JOT AND TITLE GRAVEN RED IN HUMAN BLOOD." —ELDRIDGE CLEAVER

⟨ ABE LINCOLN: AFTER THE FUNERAL ⟩

On May 4, 1865, Abraham Lincoln's body was laid to rest in a temporary vault in Oak Ridge Cemetery in Springfield, Illinois, while a permanent mausoleum was under construction. The body was moved three more times, then placed in its permanent resting place within a newly constructed granite tomb on October 15, 1874.

But in 1876 a ring of counterfeiters made two attempts to snatch Lincoln's body and hold it for ransom until an accomplice was freed from prison. The second attempt was nearly successful—it was foiled just as the conspirators were prying open the sarcophagus.

Between 1876 and 1901, Lincoln's body was moved fourteen more times—sometimes for security reasons, other times to repair the granite tomb and its dilapidated crypt. In 1901 Abe was laid to rest a final time. As his son Robert supervised, Lincoln's coffin was encased in steel bars and buried under tons of cement. The body hasn't been moved since—as far as anyone can tell.

⟨ WHICH BODY IS FRANCISCO PIZARRO'S? ⟩

Francisco Pizarro, the sixteenth-century Spanish explorer and conquistador of the Incas, was stabbed to death by his countrymen in 1541. His body was buried behind the cathedral in Lima, Peru, on the night he died, and it remained there for two and a half years. In 1544, his bones were exhumed, placed in a velvet-lined box, and deposited under the main altar of the cathedral.

Over the next 350 years, Pizarro's remains were moved repeatedly because of earthquakes and repairs to the cathedral. On the 350th anniversary of his death, in 1891, a mummified body authenticated as his was placed in a glass and marble sarcophagus, which was set out for public display. Then in 1977, some workers repairing a crypt beneath the main altar found two boxes—one lined with velvet and filled with human bones. The other box bore the Spanish inscription, "Here is the skull of the Marquis Don Francisco Pizarro, who discovered and won Peru and placed it under the crown of Castile."

Which body was Pizarro's? In 1984, forensics experts from the United States flew to Peru to compare the two sets of remains, and they determined that the bones in the velvet-lined box were those of Pizarro. His bones were then placed in a box in the glass sarcophagus, and the imposter mummy (who was never identified) was returned to the crypt underneath the altar.

⟨ JOHN PAUL JONES'S CHEAP FUNERAL ⟩

John Paul Jones, the Revolutionary War hero and founding father of the U.S. Navy, died of kidney disease and bronchial pneumonia in 1792 in Paris. Though he was one of the greatest heroes of the American Revolution, that counted for little when he died. Rather than pay to ship his body back to the U.S. for burial, the American ambassador to France instructed Jones's landlord to bury him as privately as possible and with the least amount of expense.

In 1899, 107 years later, another U.S. ambassador to France, Horace Porter, became obsessed with locating Jones's grave and returning his remains to the U.S. for a proper burial. After six years of searching, Porter was pretty sure that Jones was buried in a cemetery for Protestants. The cemetery, abandoned decades earlier, had since had an entire neighborhood built on top of it.

Acting on information that Jones had been buried in a lead casket, Porter hired a digging party to tunnel under the neighborhood and search for a lead casket among the hundreds of rotting and exposed wooden caskets. They found three lead coffins—and Jones was in the third. In fact, his body was so well preserved that it was identified by comparing its face to military medals inscribed with Jones's likeness. An American naval squadron returned him to the U.S. Naval Academy in July 1905, where the body was stored under a staircase in a dormitory for seven more years until Congress finally appropriated enough money to build a permanent crypt.

⟨ OUT OF PEP ⟩

Dale Christensen, a high school football coach in Libertyville, Illinois, once staged a fight and his own death at a pep rally to motivate the football team and fans for the game. When the community became up in arms about his "motivational skit," he resigned from his job, claiming the students and athletes simply didn't understand where he was coming from.

⟨ THE "REAL" JESSE JAMES ⟩

The Wild West bank and train robber Jesse James was shot by one of his gang members in 1882. In the years after his death, several men came forward claiming to be the real Jesse James, arguing that the person in James's grave was someone else. Finally, in 1995, the remains in James's grave were exhumed, and their

DNA was compared with that of James's living descendants. The body turned out to indeed be that of the real Jesse James.

⟨ ZACHARY TAYLOR ⟩

On July 4, 1850, Zachary Taylor, the twelfth president of the United States, ate a fresh bowl of cherries and iced milk. Hours later, he complained of stomach pains and diarrhea. On July 9, he died. Historians have always assumed that Taylor died of natural causes, but rumors that he was poisoned with arsenic never quite disappeared. Taylor opposed the extension of slavery into newly admitted states, and conspiracy theorists have speculated that he was murdered by pro-slavery forces.

In 1995, Taylor's heirs finally consented to an exhumation to settle the controversy once and for all. The tests were negative, proving that Taylor was not poisoned.

> IN LOS ANGELES IN 1976, A WOMAN LEGALLY MARRIED A 20-POUND ROCK WITH TWENTY GUESTS PRESENT.

⟨ THEY'LL SELL ANYTHING ON EBAY ⟩

In November 2006, a Michigan woman tried to sell mummified human remains on eBay. The remains, likely from a child, were once part of a Scottish anatomist's collection that came to the United States in 1820. The attempted sale was stopped, but the woman was ultimately not charged with any crime.

⟨ THE *MARY CELESTE* ⟩

The disappearance of the ship *Mary Celeste* is one of the most famous unexplained disappearances ever recorded. The vessel set off from New York on November 5, 1872, carrying a cargo of 1,701 barrels of commercial alcohol. The captain, Benjamin Spooner Briggs, was a well-known seaman who allowed no drinking on his ship and regularly read the Bible to his men. The crew had been carefully chosen for their character and seamanship, especially because the captain had brought along his wife and two-year-old daughter.

One month later, on December 5, Captain Morehouse of the *Dei Gratia*—another cargo ship—noticed a vessel on the horizon. It looked like it was in trouble, so he changed course to see if he could help. After calling out to the ship and getting no reply, Morehouse sent two of his men to board. It was immediately clear that the ship had been deserted. The ship was the *Mary Celeste*. The men looked for underwater damage, but the vessel was not leaking and was not in danger of sinking. On the whole, the *Mary Celeste* was in very good condition and should have had no problem continuing its journey. There was evidence it had been hit by a storm, but no harm was done.

The men also found that there were six months' worth of provisions and plenty of fresh water aboard the ship. All the crew's personal possessions—even their tobacco—were also still intact, indicating that the crew had left the ship in a panic, afraid for their lives. Absolutely nothing was missing, except some of the ship's papers and the ship's lifeboat. Captain Briggs, his family, and the crew had obviously abandoned the ship in a hurry. But why? What could have frightened them so much that they'd desert a seaworthy vessel for an overcrowded lifeboat and take their chances on the Atlantic?

Puzzled by the disappearance of the crew, Captain Morehouse put three men aboard the *Mary Celeste* and proceeded with both ships to Gibraltar.

Officials in Gibraltar investigated and discovered that the *Mary Celeste*'s hull was perfectly sound, indicating that she had not been in a collision. There was also no evidence of a fire or explosion. The cargo of commercial alcohol seemed to be intact and complete. The only mysterious item aboard was a sword found under the captain's bed. It seemed to have been smeared with blood, then wiped. Blood was also found on the ships railing, and both bows of the ship had strange cuts in them that could not be explained.

Solly Flood, attorney general for Gibraltar, found the bloodstains suspicious and was convinced that there had been violence aboard the *Mary Celeste*. Morehouse and his crew were cleared of any suspicion, and after the ship's owners had paid Morehouse a reward, the ship was given a new crew and went on to Italy, where its cargo was delivered. It continued to sail for twelve years, but was always known as a hoodoo ship, so most seamen refused to set foot on her.

To this day, no one knows what exactly happened aboard the *Mary Celeste*, but people all over the world have theories. Some believe a mutiny had occurred—the crew murdered the captain and his family, then took the ship. But why would they abandon their prize? There is the possibility that pirates attacked the ship and killed everyone on it. But that theory makes no sense because nothing was stolen. Perhaps an outbreak of disease panicked those left alive, but why would they subject themselves to the close quarters of a smaller boat, where crowding would ensure that everyone caught the disease? The most outrageous explanation is that the ship had been attacked by a giant squid, several times, until everyone was killed. But a squid wouldn't have been interested in the ship's papers, and it wouldn't need the ship's lifeboat.

Experts say only one feasible explanation has been proposed. This theory postulates that four things happened, in succession: First, the captain died of natural causes while the ship was caught in bad weather. Then a crew member misread the depth of the water in the hold, and everyone panicked, thinking the ship was going down. They abandoned the ship in such a hurry that they took no food or water, and everyone in the lifeboat either starved or drowned.

Is this what happened? Maybe, but we'll never know for sure.

The bubonic plague was nicknamed the Black Death because of the nasty black sores it left on its victims' bodies.

⟨ THE GHOST SHIP ⟩

Nautical lore is rife with stories of ghost ships. One of the oldest and most celebrated of these stories, the tale of the *Sarah*, started with a lover's quarrel.

The year was 1812, and two young sailors, George Leverett and Charles Jose, set out from their native Portland, Maine, to South Freeport to build and stock a ship they planned to use for trading in the Indies. It was there that the pair met and fell in love with Sarah Soule. Both men vied for the lady's attention, but in the end it was Leverett who won her hand in marriage. Dejected and angry, Jose disappeared.

It wasn't until Leverett was married and his rig, the *Sarah*, was sailing due south that Jose reemerged— as captain of an unmarked ship that was trailing the *Sarah*. Spooked, Leverett and his crew changed course, hoping to report Jose to the British admiralty, but they never made it. Jose's ship fired its cannons, killing all of the other ship's crew and nearly sinking the *Sarah*. Miraculously, Leverett was not killed, so the vengeful Jose jumped onto the deck of the *Sarah*, tied the captain to the mast, and set him out to sea.

Leverett resigned himself to death—he was floating on an open sea in an unmanned and badly damaged vessel. It was then that the truly astonishing began to happen. Leverett watched, horrified, as his crew slowly came back to life, resuming their posts one by one. The pale and silent crew then started guiding the ship toward home. Leverett lost consciousness.

The ghost crew sailed the ship safely all the way to Pott's Point, Wales. Onlookers from the shore reported that one foggy day, a dilapidated but fully rigged ship materialized from the gloom and came to a full stop. An apparently lifeless man was then lowered from the ship onto a smaller boat and rowed to shore. The crew, silent and pallid, never said a word. Once their cargo was safely laid on a rock, they returned to the ship and slowly sailed away. The ship was never to be seen again. Captain Leverett regained consciousness and lived to tell the tale.

⟨ BRITISH WITCHES STOP HITLER'S ARMY ⟩

When he learned that Adolf Hitler planned to invade England, British prime minister Neville Chamberlain went to Munich, Germany, in September 1938 to stop him. He returned to England with a treaty declaring there would be "peace for our time." Widely accused of appeasing the Nazis, he was voted out of office. A year later, when Hitler invaded Poland, World War II began.

In May and June of 1940, the British Expeditionary Force was nearly crushed by the Nazi army. What saved them was what Winston Churchill called a "miracle of deliverance." More than three hundred thousand men were rescued from the coastal town of Dunkirk, France, and brought back across the English Channel by English civilians in every kind of boat—yachts, fishing boats, pleasure boats, even rowboats.

On July 31, 1940, it is said that English witches gathered in the New Forest, in Hampshire, and raised a monumental cone of power to stop Hitler's forces. It is also said that the well-known witch Gerald Gardner and his coven joined this grand coven. Five of Gardner's coveners died a few days later, and Gardner reported that he had been weakened by the energy.

⟨ THE SALEM WITCH TRIALS ⟩

It all began in Salem, Massachusetts, in January of 1692, when two girls, Elizabeth Parris and Abigail Williams, began to show unusual symptoms: screaming, convulsions, and trancelike behavior. The doctor declared that their fits could only mean that the girls were under the influence of witches.

Soon many more girls throughout Salem were complaining of similar symptoms. They jumped into holes, crept under chairs, and contorted their bodies in all kinds of odd ways. Others, especially in the company of one particular minister, would make odd sounds, and some even pulled burning logs from fireplaces and threw them around the room.

People prayed. People fasted. The fits continued anyway. Fingers were pointed to the weakest and strangest of the village, such as Tituba, a slave from Barbados; Sarah Good, a beggar; and Sarah Osborne, an old bedridden woman.

But as panic grew and the fits continued, more people were accused of being witches, including the Goodwife Proctor, whose husband was a successful farmer and tavern keeper. Also accused was Martha Cory, the wife of a farmer and landowner; the governor's wife; and even Dorcas Good, a four-year-old girl!

A special court was established in Salem to hear the cases against the accused, and the trials began in June. Bridget Bishop was the first to be tried and hanged.

In the end, hundreds were accused, and 150 were imprisoned and chained to the prison walls. In all, twenty people were executed, and more perished in prison.

‹ KILLING WITCHES ›

We all know that witches were burned at the stake, but it turns out that in Salem, Massachusetts, the famous witchcraft capital of New England, other methods were preferred. Twenty-five witches died in Salem: nineteen died by hanging, four died waiting in prison, and one was crushed to death using large stones.

‹ LADY GODIVA'S RIDE ›

In 1040, Leonfric, earl of Mercia and lord of Coventry, laid such onerous taxes on the people that they were starving. When Lady Godiva, his wife, begged him to be merciful, he challenged her. If she would ride naked through the town, he would rescind the taxes. Godiva ordered that all windows be covered at noon and that all townspeople stay indoors. She mounted her white stallion and rode through the town, her long hair her only garment. Only one man dared to look at her; his name has come down to us as Peeping Tom. He was struck blind. It is said that his eyes shriveled into darkness at the moment he beheld Godiva's naked figure.

Godiva was not just any medieval English noblewoman. The tale of Lady Godiva is the story of a (Celtic?) goddess, possibly Epona, who road naked on a white horse while she bestowed blessings upon her people—on their houses and work, their fields and crops.

⟨ A TRULY TERRIBLE TV MOMENT ⟩

The host of a talk show in Florida, Christine Chubbock, signed off her show on July 15, 1974, by remarking that her viewers were about to see a TV first. She then presented a gun and killed herself on camera.

Franklin Delano Roosevelt, the thirty-second president of the United States, and Dick Cheney, the forty-sixth vice president, share the same birthday: January 30.

⟨ TAKING TV TOO SERIOUSLY ⟩

A couple in Toronto fought so viciously over who was the prettier actress on the TV sitcom *Married With Children* (Christina Applegate or Katey Segal) that the wife slashed the husband in the crotch with a broken wine bottle. They eventually made up, only to get into the same fight again. The second time, she broke his shoulder and arm, and he stabbed her multiple times.

BIZARRE AND BRUTAL ROYALTY

▸❯ TINY ENEMIES ❮◂

Queen Christina of Sweden, who ruled in the 1600s, had a tiny problem—she was absolutely terrified of fleas. She was so afraid, in fact, that she commissioned the construction of a tiny cannon for her bedroom, which used to fire itty-bitty cannonballs at the pesky critters. No word on how good a shot she was, but apparently it was an activity that she spent hours per day on.

▸❯ BLOODY MARY ❮◂

Queen Mary I of England and Ireland (1516–1558) was a Catholic who had Protestants tortured and killed. Her actions inspired the nickname Bloody Mary, which in turn inspired the cocktail.

▸❯ ONE LUCKY FLOWER ❮◂

Russia's Catherine the Great (1729–1796) once saw a primrose in her garden and fell in love with it, setting a guard over it to protect it from harm.

▶▸❯ PRINCESS DELUSIONAL ❮◂◀

When she was a child, Princess Alexandria of Bavaria (1826–1875) became convinced that she had swallowed a grand piano.

▶▸❯ ENDURING LOVE ❮◂◀

Spanish Queen Juana so loved her husband, Philip, that when he passed away in 1506, she kept his coffin with her for the rest of her life, refusing to allow him to be buried.

▶▸❯ A DEADLY MARRIAGE ❮◂◀

Princess Maria del Pozzo della Cisterno's 1867 wedding day was a bad one, but not because of fiancé Amadeo, the future king of Italy. It was everyone else that caused the trouble: her wardrobe mistress hanged herself, the gatekeeper cut his throat, someone got caught under the wheels of the honeymoon train and died, an associate of the king fell from his horse to his death, and the best man shot himself.

❮ POOR RICH CHILD ❯

Isabella, daughter of Charles VI of France, was a true child bride. She was wed in 1396 at age seven to twenty-nine-year-old King Richard II of England to cement a political alliance. Just three years later, in 1399, Richard was usurped by King Henry IV and died in 1400, leaving Isabella a widow at the tender age of ten.

⟨ SECRETS OF THE VOYNICH MANUSCRIPT ⟩

The Voynich manuscript is a mystery that has puzzled scholars for hundreds of years. Wilfrid Voynich, a collector of rare books and manuscripts, acquired the 246-page, intricately illustrated manuscript at a Jesuit college in Frascati, Italy, in 1912. The earliest confirmed owner was Georg Baresch, an obscure alchemist who lived in Prague in the early seventeenth century.

Believed to date from the late Middle Ages or the Renaissance period, the Voynich manuscript is written in a language and script that has yet to be deciphered by the scores of linguists, cryptographers, and historians who have attempted to crack it. The text contains about 35,000 "words," derived from what seems to be an alphabet of twenty to thirty distinct glyphs, although some of the glyphs appear only once or twice. The words and glyphs are unlike any others known in linguistic history. Equally curious are the images—the manuscript is densely illustrated with drawings of unknown botanical and pharmaceutical specimens and curious astronomical diagrams. Although nobody knows who wrote the manuscript, it has been attributed to sixteenth-century English mathematician and astrologer John Dee, Dee's companion Edward Kelley, and even to Voynich himself.

In the sixteenth century, Lady Glamis was accused of witchcraft and trying to murder the king of Scotland. She was burned at the stake. Her ghost now haunts Glamis Castle in Angus, Scotland. Many visitors have seen her floating above the clock tower.

⟨ NOT JUST A TRAIN STATION ⟩

King's Cross station, located in the heart of London, is not just a train station—it's also the rumored burial place of the ancient warrior queen Boudicca, leader of the Iceni people of Norfolk in eastern Britain. In A.D. 60 or 61, she led a rebellion against the occupying forces of the Roman Empire, marching from Colchester and St. Albans to London, where she was defeated at Battle Bridge, the site that is now known as King's Cross station.

THE BOOK OF THE BIZARRE

⟨ OTTO WAS BLOTTO ⟩

Despite being king of Bavaria for nearly thirty years, Otto of Bavaria never really reigned over his kingdom. Crowned after the strange and unexpected death of his brother in 1886, Otto had been declared insane years earlier, and by some accounts wasn't even aware that he was king. Otto's uncle and cousin served as prince regents and made most of the kingly decisions for him.

⟨ BYE BYE BIRDIE ⟩

General Richard Ewell served the Confederacy well, but he was a touch eccentric in his personal life. His men reported that the general, well known for his delusions, fancied himself a bird, eating seeds and grains for meals and spending long hours inside his tent, chirping.

Andrew Jackson, seventh president of the United States, suffered from habitual slobbering during his childhood and teens.

⟨ MAGIC MUMMY POWDER ⟩

Twelfth-century Egypt was full of mummies. The ancient custom of mummifying everything from people to dogs to bulls to birds created a mummy-excess problem —mummies were buried under houses, farms, public arenas, you name it. It wasn't until Islam began to take hold that the idea of disposing of mummified bodies became acceptable, and Egyptians responded by burning scores of mummies for fuel. Mummies were also dug up and ground into a fine powder, appropriately called mummy powder, which was known as a kind of panacea for everything from nausea to epilepsy to paralysis. The powder was even used as an additive in paints, as it was believed it prevented color from fading.

⟨ NO RESPECT FOR ELDERS ⟩

Ninth-century Pope Formosus made a few notable enemies during his lifetime. One of them, his successor, Pope Stephen VI, couldn't put the past behind him and forgive Formosus for the injustices he felt the former pope had imposed on him. Stephen had his orderlies dig up the dead pope, dress him in robes, and put his corpse on trial. And because the corpse could not exactly speak for itself, he had a young deacon kneel behind the body and act as Formosus's impersonator.

Former U.S. president Gerald Ford changed his name when he was twenty-two—a good thing, because his birth name was Leslie Lynch King, Jr.

⟨ THE MYSTERY OF THE CARNAC STONES ⟩

Everyone knows about Stonehenge, the prehistoric monument of stones located in the English countryside. Lesser known but just as extraordinary are the Carnac Stones, a collection of more than 3,000 freestanding megaliths that can be found in the area outside the French village of Carnac, in Brittany. The stones, which stand in straight columns measuring hundreds of meters long, are the subject of many theories and much speculation. One myth posits that they are the remains of a Roman legion that Merlin, the wizard of the Arthurian legend, turned to stone. They are thought to date from between 3300 and 4500 B.C. The stones are remarkable for their organization and their incredible size; one stone, known as the Giant, is 6.5 meters tall.

⟨ AND WE THOUGHT SPITTOONS WERE BAD ⟩

The Romans believed that purging the digestive system was very important to the overall health of the body. As such, they built special "vomitoriums," where wealthy Romans could lose their lunch, clean up, and settle in for their next gourmet meal.

UNUSUAL CUSTOMS

▶❯ BEE AROUND ❮◀

It was once tradition in old England, upon the death of a family member, to find the nearest beehive and tell the bees about the death. Doing so was thought to prevent the bees from abandoning their hive.

▶❯ BAD NEWS FOR CHOCOHOLICS ❮◀

In villages in Central America during the eighteenth century, chocolate was believed to be the drink of the devil, and no one under sixty was allowed to imbibe under threat of excommunication from the Catholic Church.

MIRROR, MIRROR

Mirrors ward off evil spirits—or so thought the ancient Chinese, who were convinced that spirits did not want to be seen in a looking glass.

⟨ THE CUMAEAN SIBYL ⟩

Ancient Rome had ten Sibyls—prophetesses who channeled divine energy—who lived in Persia, Libya, Samos, Cimmeria, Erythraea, Tibur, Marpessus, Phrygia, Delphi, and Cumae. One of the best known is the Cumaean Sibyl, who lived near Naples in the fifth century B.C. Her cave, which was said to lead directly to the underworld, was rediscovered in 1932; the passageway is 375 feet long. Like the priestess at Delphi, the Cumaean Sibyl gained her powers through association with the god Apollo, who offered her anything if she would spend the night with him. She asked for eternal life, but as she neglected to ask for eternal youth, she shriveled into a shadow.

She wrote her prophecies on leaves that she placed at the mouth of her cave. If no one came to pick them up, she let the wind scatter them. *The Sibylline Verses*, which told the Romans how to gain favor with foreign gods, were eventually bound into nine volumes, which the Sibyl tried to sell to the Roman king, Tarquin. He scoffed at the high price, so she burned three of the books. The price was still too high, he scoffed again, and she burned three more books. When she returned with the last three books, the king decided maybe there was something he ought to know, so he bought them. They were kept in the capitol and consulted until some were destroyed in a fire in 83 B.C. The rest survived until another fire in A.D. 405, at which time enterprising Romans began writing pseudo-Sibylline prophecies.

⤙ AS THE BIRD TOLLS ⤚

Ancient Romans never made a decision without first observing the flight patterns of the birds that soared above their empire. This practice was so valuable that in very early times areas were cleared of buildings and trees so as not to obscure the view of the birds' flights. The augur would perform a divination ceremony, marking off space in the sky with his staff and taking note of the birds' direction, speed, and song, whenever an important military or political decision was to be made.

⟨ FORTUNA REDUX ⟩

Fortuna Redux was the Roman goddess of successful journeys and safe returns. She has been probably invoked, if only unconsciously, by every explorer who ever set foot on unknown land.

Emperor Augustus erected an altar to Fortuna Redux after he returned from a long journey through Asia in 19 B.C. In A.D. 93 a new temple was erected by the emperor Domitian, who was forever doing battle to keep the empire together and himself on the throne.

⟨ THE EVIL EYE ⟩

The concept of the evil eye dates back to around 3000 B.C. Mentioned in the Bible and ancient Sumerian, Assyrian, and Voudon texts, it is still prevalent in parts of Europe, Central America, and Mexico. Historical notions of the evil eye fall into two categories. The intentional category assumes that the perpetrators—such as witches, warlocks, and medicine men—purposely cast their evil eyes over their victims. But some unfortunate souls are afflicted with the evil eye without even knowing it, and the people around them must learn to avoid their wicked gazes or risk death, destruction, or despair. Two notable figures said to have been born with the evil eye were Pope Pius IX and Pope Leo XIII.

- A grilled-cheese sandwich bearing the image of the Virgin Mary was sold in 2004 for $28,000.
- Ancient Bulgarians insisted that one finish one's entire meal before leaving the dinner table. This custom supposedly encouraged the hens to sit patiently on their nests and brood.
- The ancient Romans took great stock in the wisdom of astrology. Emperor Tiberius consulted with his personal astrologer before making any key decision.

⟨ HAIL MARY ⟩

"Marian apparition" is the fancy term for the appearance or manifestation of the Virgin Mary. Most of these apparitions appear as gleaming specters that may encourage prayer and church building, perform miraculous healings, or put people into trances. The apparitions have often appeared around churches, such as the St. Mary's Coptic church in Zeitoun, Egypt, where there had been more than seventy appearances in a fourteen-month period, beginning in 1968. One of the appearances lasted for over seven hours and was witnessed by hundreds of people.

⟨ KEEP YOUR EARS CLOSED ⟩

Ancient Mesopotamians believed that the gods dictated each person's life span before their birth, and that there was nothing one could do, good or bad, to extend or shorten it. At death one transformed into a spirit or ghost, and those who had experienced violent deaths would enter living beings through their ears, causing grief and illness until the spirit was exorcised—a particularly violent practice itself.

⟨ EVIL-BLASTING BEAUTY ⟩

The ancients wore eye shadow to prevent blindness, strengthen eyesight, and offer protection. Meanwhile, eyeliner was said to keep out evil, and lipstick, to guard against evil spirits and poisonous foods, and to keep the soul from leaving the body through the breath.

4. TENDER MURDERERS
AND MALEVOLENT MALES

KILLINGLY GOOD TALES OF TERROR

"Wild animals never kill for sport. Man is the only one to whom the torture and death of his fellow creatures is amusing in itself." —JAMES ANTHONY FROUDE

⟨ LOCUSTA THE POISONOUS ⟩

Those who control the cooking always have the opportunity to slip a little something extra into the stew. And the most famous fiendish cook of all was the Roman royal Locusta, who poisoned the emperor Claudius about 2,000 years ago, so that her son Nero could become emperor. Stories about what method she used vary; some say poisonous mushrooms, others say mushrooms laced with poison. Either way, she accomplished her mission.

⟨ SWEENEY TODD ⟩

A villain appearing in numerous English legends in the nineteenth century, Sweeney Todd may not be an entirely fictitious character. Scholar Peter Haining argues that Sweeney Todd was a real historical figure who did, in fact, commit crimes during the 1800s. The story, as it has now become legendary, is as follows:

Sweeney Todd had a barbershop on London's Fleet Street, right next door to St. Dunstan's Church. His shop was a simple one-room affair, having a single barber chair located in the middle of the floor. But Sweeney had rigged up an ingenious device: the chair was connected to a trapdoor beneath it, and when Sweeney had a wealthy customer and the coast was clear, he'd pull a lever that sent customer and chair dropping through the trapdoor into his basement. At the same time, another barber chair would pop up to take the place of the one in the cellar, so that at no time was the shop without a chair.

Meanwhile, Sweeney would run hell-bent-for-leather down to the basement. If the fall hadn't killed his victim, Sweeney would help him along into the next world by slitting his throat. Then he'd strip the corpse, taking everything valuable, and expertly carve up the body like a butcher. The human flesh would be delivered to his accomplice and lover, Mrs. Margery Lovett, who ran a meat-pie shop on Bell Lane. Little did the customers know that the meat in the pies wasn't pork, beef, or chicken, but human.

As for the body parts that weren't worthy of pies—the bones, skin, and heads—Sweeney had discovered a tunnel and catacombs beneath the church, and there, among the burial vaults of long-dead parishioners, he distributed the grisly remains of his victims. Sweeney met his downfall when the parishioners of St. Dunston's began to notice a foul odor coming from below. A search of the tunnels revealed the ghastly rotting remains, and bloody footprints led back to Sweeney's barbershop and Mrs. Lovett's pie place. When her customers realized what she had been feeding them, they tried to lynch her then and there, but the London police managed to save her, and Sweeney, for the gallows.

⟨ CREEPY VENGEANCE ⟩

Catherine, the wife of Russian czar Peter I, had a wandering eye, and Peter caught on. To teach Catherine a lesson, he forced her to watch her lover be killed, then pickled the lover's head and kept it in their bedroom.

⟨ PRESIDENTIAL POISONING? ⟩

Did Florence Harding kill her husband, U.S. president Warren G. Harding, while he was still in office?

Rumors persist. It all started with allegations of an affair. While he was president, there were stories that Harding had fathered a child with a much younger woman. Mrs. Harding got the FBI on the case to put the rumor to rest. Agents discovered it was true, which peeved Florence to no end. She then inquired of the FBI about killing someone by putting an undetectable white powder in their food. What was that powder? she asked. They refused to tell her. Soon after, the president got sick with what was believed to be food poisoning—no one else got sick, although they all ate the same thing—and died. Mrs. Harding refused to allow an autopsy, and the death was officially regarded as a stroke.

⊰ ODD BEAUTY TREATMENTS ⊱

One of the most prolific murderers of all time was one Elizabeth Bathori, who lived in the 1600s in Transylvania. She is reputed to have killed more than 600 women and girls to drink and bathe in their blood, which she believed would keep her young. The niece of the king of Poland, she was not killed when the murders were discovered, but instead was walled up in her castle until her death.

⟨ JUSTICE WILL PREVAIL (EVENTUALLY) ⟩

In 1806, Becky Cotton, of Edgefield, South Carolina, was tried for murdering her third husband with an ax. When authorities dredged the pond to find her husband's body, they also discovered the bodies of Cotton's two previous husbands—one dead from poisoning and the other with a large needle stuck straight through his heart. An eyewitness account of her trial recalls: "As she stood at the bar in tears, with cheeks like rosebuds wet with morning dew and rolling her eyes of living sapphires, pleading for pity, their subtle glamour seized with ravishment the admiring bar—the stern features of justice were all relaxed, and the judge and jury hanging forward from their seats were heard to exclaim, 'Heavens! What a charming creature.'"

Cotton was found innocent and promptly married a jury member. But justice did prevail eventually—her brother murdered her.

⟨ THE MURDER IN THE RED BARN ⟩

This much sensationalized and notorious murder took place in Polstead, near Ipswich, England, and achieved immortality in its many retellings. Maria, the daughter of a local mole-catcher, was known about the village as a woman of loose morals. She bore an illegitimate son to Thomas Corder, the son of a wealthy local farmer. Later William Corder, Thomas's younger brother, became enamored of Maria, and eventually arranged to meet her in May of 1827 in the red barn on the family's farm, so they could travel together to Ipswich and get married. All accounts indicate that though Maria was seen heading to the barn, she was never seen again after that. In 1828 Maria's body was discovered in the red barn, and William Corder was hanged for her murder.

⟨ RAH RAH SIS BOOM BAH! ⟩

Wanda Webb Holloway, a Channelview, Texas, housewife, was just trying to be a good mother to her eighth-grade daughter, Shanna Harper, who was trying out for the school's cheerleading squad and facing stiff competition in Amber Heath, a classmate who had gotten a spot on the squad two years in a row. Holloway had the idea that if she could have Heath's mother "taken care of," the girl would be so grief stricken she would drop out of cheerleading, assuring Holloway's daughter of the plum cheerleading spot.

So Holloway hired and conspired with a hit man, actually her ex-brother-in-law, even giving him a pair of diamond earrings as a down payment. But police got wind of the scheme before it could be carried out, and in September 1991, she was arrested for solicitation of murder.

⟨ THE AMY FISHER STORY ⟩

Amy Fisher led a charmed life—wealthy parents, luxurious Long Island home, her own phone line—but the Jewish-Italian princess had a dark past. When she was twelve, she was raped by the man who had been hired to retile her family's bathroom floor, and she was afraid to tell anyone—least of all her father, who was prone to violent rages.

In 1991, when Amy totaled the white Dodge her father had bought her for her sixteenth birthday, Daddy took the car—and Amy—to Complete Auto Body and Fender Repair to get it fixed. It was there that sixteen-year-old Amy met Joey Buttafuoco, head mechanic and lady-killer.

The two felt a mutual attraction, and despite Joey's wife and two kids and Amy's tender age, they jumped headfirst into a torrid affair. They had sex in hotel rooms, in Amy's house, and on Joey's boat. At Joey's suggestion, Amy started working for ABBA escort service as a prostitute; she was so popular that she took her business freelance after a couple months. She started sleeping with other men, but Joey didn't care—he was in it for the sex, which was apparently really, really good. Amy, on the other hand, loved Joey and begged him to leave his wife, which he refused to do.

Amy wouldn't take no for an answer. After all, she'd grown up rich and privileged, and she was used to getting what she wanted. She wondered what would happen if Joey's wife, Mary Jo Buttafuoco, suddenly disappeared—and she then decided to make it happen. Amy promised Peter Guagenti, a Brooklyn College dropout, $800 and sex in exchange for use of his .25 handgun. On May 19, 1992, she went to the high school nurse's office and claimed she was sick and had to go home early. Peter picked her up in his Thunderbird, drove her to the Buttafuoco home, and handed her the gun.

Mary Jo answered the door wearing her sweats—she was painting some lawn furniture. After a brief conversation in which Amy claimed that her sixteen-year-old sister was having an affair with Joey, Mary Jo asked Amy to leave and retreated into the house. Before the door could swing shut, Amy had shot her in the head, severing Mary Jo's carotid artery.

The rest is history, well documented in myriad made-for-TV movies, books, and Web sites dedicated to the Amy Fisher story. In fact, Amy posted bail (for a whopping $2 million) with the money she earned from TV and book deals. She was sentenced to five to fifteen years in prison, and Joey spent four months in jail for statutory rape. As for Mary Jo, she survived, despite major paralysis on one half of her face.

⟨ INDIANA OGRESS ⟩

Belle Gunness was very practical. She murdered for money. Belle's first husband, Mads Sorenson, opened a confectioner's shop with her in 1896. The business didn't do well, and it burned down. Luckily, the couple had insurance. They bought several houses, each of which also burned down. Luckily, the houses were insured. Two of the couple's babies died—of acute colitis, said the doctors. The children had been insured. And then in 1900, Mads died from what the doctors decided was a heart attack. Belle collected on his two insurance policies totaling $8,000.

Belle took the money and her remaining kids, including a foster daughter, Jennie Olson, and bought a two-story brick farmhouse in LaPorte, Indiana. In

1902, Belle was married again, to a farmer named Peter Gunness. Peter, a widower, brought along his baby, who died a week after the wedding. Peter lasted about a year, before a heavy iron sausage grinder fell onto his head from a top shelf. Daughter Myrtle confided to a school chum that Mama had conked Papa on the noggin and killed him, but nobody paid attention. Belle collected Peter's $3,000 insurance policy and dressed herself in mourning black—but not for long.

Soon Belle was placing ads in Scandinavian newspapers across the Midwest, seeking a husband. "Widow with large farm looking for a helpmate," the ads went, adding that it was important that the prospective groom produce money of his own, so that she would know he wasn't merely a cad after her fortune. Corresponding with hopeful suitors, she would ask them to bring with them a sum of at least $1,000 to prove their sincerity.

Ole Busberg, Olaf Lindbloom, Herman Konitzer, Emil Tell, Olaf Jensen, Charles Nieberg, Tonnes Lien, and who knows how many other Olafs, Oles, and Erics came to LaPorte to woo Belle. Trouble was, none of them stayed. Belle would be seen with each man around town for a few days, hanging on his arm and adding his money to her bank account, then suddenly he'd be gone—gone back to Minnesota, gone back to Sweden, she would say.

Plowing her fields while wearing the coat and hat the man had left behind, she'd bemoan her lot: she was a poor widow, deserted by another scoundrel who loved her and dumped her. And another ad would appear in the lonely hearts section of the *Scandinavian News*.

Somewhere along the way, Jennie Olson disappeared too. Belle told the neighbors that her foster daughter had gone to an exclusive girls' finishing school in California.

Finally, in January 1908, Andrew Helgelein showed up in LaPorte, bringing with him $1,000 as proof of his good intentions. Helgelein had the "good luck" to disappear, like the others. But when his brother, Asa, hadn't heard from Andrew in some months, he wrote to Belle. Belle wrote back, saying Andrew had returned to the Old Country. Asa didn't buy it. He announced that he was coming to LaPorte to see for himself.

On April 27, 1908, Belle visited a lawyer. A farmhand whom she had fired, Ray Lamphere, was harassing her, she said, and just in case anything happened to her, she wanted to make a will, leaving her money to her children.

In the early morning hours of April 28, Belle's farmhouse burned to the ground. Found in the ashes were the burned bodies of Belle and her three children. Ray Lamphere, the disgruntled farmhand (and also Belle's sometime lover), was arrested for arson and murder.

There was one problem: the body presumed to be Belle's was missing its head. Even without the head, it was obvious that this corpse was much smaller and lighter than the hefty widow. Then Asa Helgelein showed up in town, suspecting foul play in his brother's disappearance and asking permission to dig around the farm.

On May 5, the first body was uncovered. It was brother Andrew, with fatal doses of arsenic and strychnine in his stomach. Quickly, the digging crew uncovered more bodies, including that of Jennie Olson. All in all, at least thirteen bodies were dug up, but the final estimate was higher than that, perhaps forty, because of the numerous bone fragments found in the pigpen. Belle had been feeding her suitors' bodies to the pigs.

Ray Lamphere was found guilty only of arson, because it was impossible to prove whether or not the headless corpse was Belle. He was sent to prison for two to twenty years and died there of tuberculosis two years later, still insisting that Belle was alive somewhere.

He wasn't the only person who believed she was alive. Sightings of Belle became as common as UFO sightings would be seventy years later. In fact, a woman fitting her description was connected to a 1931 murder in California, where Belle was believed to have fled after the fire.

⟨ THE FRANKIE SILVER STORY ⟩

Frankie Silver was the first woman to be hung in the state of North Carolina. She killed her husband, Charlie Silver, on December 22, 1831.

Frankie, born Frances Stewart, had been a young girl of about seventeen years old when she married Charlie Silver, who was probably all of eighteen. It was a hard life that they lived, and within a year, Frankie had given birth to a baby girl. Her life was miserable. The Silvers lived in an isolated area, miles from the nearest town, and Charlie had a habit of leaving his young wife alone for days at a time while he was off drinking and chasing women. To add to Frankie's misery, when Charlie came home drunk, he was abusive. Everyone knew that Charlie beat Frankie. They may not have approved, but wife beating was an accepted practice in those days. There was the unwritten, but accepted law that was called "rule of thumb," which said that a man shouldn't beat his wife with a stick that was wider than his thumb. Charlie, it was said, broke the rule.

On December 23, 1831, Frankie came to the house where Charlie's family lived to tell them that Charlie hadn't been home for days. Their cabin was cold, she'd burned up all the firewood, and she was taking the baby and going home to her folks. She didn't care if Charlie never came home again. Charlie's family searched the woods and river for him, thinking maybe he'd fallen through the ice or been attacked by an animal.

Finally, Charlie's father hiked forty miles across the mountains to Tennessee, where there lived a slave who, folks said, could "conjure." The slave was gone, but his master used the conjure ball, a ball on a string that moved like a pendulum, over a map that Charlie's father had drawn. It stopped right over the crude sketch of Charlie's cabin. That's where to look for Charlie, said the man.

Meanwhile, a neighbor, Jack Collis, explored the abandoned cabin. He noticed that there was an extraordinary amount of ash in the fireplace; Frankie's last fire seemed to have consumed a huge amount of wood and burned very hot and very long. The ashes were suspiciously greasy. Poking around in the fireplace, Collis discovered bits of human bone. Neighbors pried up the floorboards and found a puddle of blood "large as a hog's liver." Next, the family and friends searched around outside the house and found grisly parts of Charlie—parts that wouldn't burn—hidden all over. In a recently dug hole filled with ashes was the iron heel of one of his hunting shoes. A hollow tree stump concealed his liver and heart. Charlie's family buried the body parts as quickly as they found them. When they found more parts, instead of opening the grave, they dug a new grave. As a result, Charlie Silver has three graves.

On January 10, 1832, Frankie was arrested for the murder of her husband. But there was a problem: Frankie stood four feet, ten inches high, and Charlie was big, weighing twice as much as she. How could she have dragged his body to the fireplace and chopped it up herself? She had to have had help. Her mother and her brother were arrested, only to be released for lack of evidence. Frankie was brought to trial alone, and within two days she was found guilty and sentenced to be hanged. The prosecution—and the legend—accused her of hacking up Charlie and burning his pieces out of jealousy for his affairs with other women. Frankie never got to tell her side of the story because she was not allowed to testify.

⊰ LIZZIE BORDEN'S FORTY WHACKS ⊱

In August 1892, spinster Lizzie Borden was thirty-two years old, and her sister Emma was forty. The Borden family, including the girls' father, Andrew, and their stepmother, Abby, lived in a dark, cramped wooden house in a shabby neighborhood in Fall River,

Massachusetts. The only running water came from the kitchen sink, and the only toilet was located in the cellar. They didn't even own a horse and buggy.

Andrew Borden was, ironically, a retired undertaker and very rich. But he also was a miser. He had married plain, heavyset Abby because he needed a wife and unpaid housekeeper. Emma and Lizzie refused to call her Mother.

Lizzie experienced some severe trauma in her childhood. For example, she loved animals and kept a coop of pigeons in the family's barn. When small boys started breaking into the barn, presumably to get at the pigeons, Andrew Borden's solution was to chop the heads off all the birds. Lizzie later recalled asking her father, "Where are their heads?"

Perhaps her father's cruelty to her pigeons fueled Lizzie's own inherent cruelty, or perhaps the trauma of the pigeon experience merely hardened Lizzie's heart, for not long after, Lizzie chopped off the head of her step-mother's cat. The cat had pushed open the door to Lizzie's bedroom, where Lizzie had been entertaining guests. Lizzie carried the cat downstairs, put its little head on the chopping block, and chopped it off. For days Abby wondered where her cat had gone. Finally Lizzie told her, "You go downstairs, and you'll find your cat."

On the morning of August 4, 1892, while Andrew was out checking on one of his businesses and Emma was away visiting friends, Lizzie told the Borden's maid, Bridget, that her stepmother had gone off to see a sick friend. Later in the morning, Andrew returned home, carrying a small parcel wrapped in paper. It contained a broken lock that he had picked off the floor of one of his properties. Bridget opened the door for him, and as she stood at the entrance, letting him in, she heard a sound that was very unusual in the Borden house. Lizzie Borden was standing at the top of the stairs, laughing out loud.

Like a solicitous daughter, Lizzie helped her father relax on the dark horsehair sofa, so that he could nap. She pulled off his shoes and folded his coat under his head for a pillow. She then told Bridget about a sale of goods at the local shop, perhaps to get her out of the house. Bridget said she'd go later and climbed the stairs to her little attic room to lie down for a while. She was roused shortly after 11 A.M. by Lizzie's shout, "Come down! Father's dead!"

Bridget and Lizzie quickly called for doctors and friends galore, and by 11:45, there was a crowd gathered outside the house. The doctor, after examining Andrew Borden's gory remains, asked for a sheet to cover the body.

Lizzie answered, "Better get two."

And where was Mrs. Borden? First Lizzie repeated the story that her stepmother had gone to see a sick friend. Then she added that she might have heard Abby come in and that maybe she was upstairs. Bridget and another woman climbed the stairs to find Abby, with her head crushed in, lying in a pool of congealed blood on the floor of the upstairs guest bedroom. During the funeral, the police searched Lizzie's closet for a bloodstained dress, to no avail. The following week, she was arrested for the murder of her father and stepmother.

Although there was great evidence that could prove Lizzie was the murderer, she was acquitted. The jury saw her as too much of a lady to have committed such a gruesome crime. After the trial, Lizzie and Emma, now rich, bought themselves a fourteen-room mansion in a neighborhood called the Hill, where the rest of the gentry lived. Though it was never proved, the rest of the gentry living up on the Hill had to wonder, did Lizzie Borden kill her father by hitting him with an axe ten times and her stepmother nineteen? And could she have hit them hard enough to crush Abby Borden's skull, slice Andrew's eye in half, sever his nose, and render his face into an unrecognizable pulp? They never bothered to find out. They didn't care to socialize with Lizzie Borden—not one bit.

"Lacking ladylike poison, Lizzie (Borden) did what every over-civilized, understated Wasp is entirely capable of doing once we finally admit we're mad as hell and aren't going to take it any more: She went from Anglo to Saxon in a trice." —FLORENCE KING

⟨ ONE MORE REASON TO FEAR CLOWNS ⟩

John Wayne Gacy was an overweight, unattractive man with a passion for raping and murdering young males. Like so many other serial killers, Gacy had delusions, or at least dreams of grandeur. He wanted to be a local icon, so he joined local political groups, threw parties, and dressed as a clown named Pogo to entertain the local kids. His efforts were well received, and he was popular with children and parents alike, until authorities found the bodies of scores of neighborhood boys buried in his basement. In 1980, a jury convicted Mr. Gacy of murdering thirty-three young men, and he was executed fourteen years later.

⟨ NO WILLY WONKA ⟩

Jeffrey Dahmer was known to be a calm, articulate man working in a chocolate factory in Milwaukee. In reality, he was a murdering, cannibalistic sociopath. In 1989 he was arrested for molesting children, and in 1991 he was arrested for the murder of thirteen men and sentenced to 957 years in prison.

⟨ A MURDERING MADAME ⟩

Patty Cannon was a large woman, said to be equal to a man when it came down to a fight. In the early 1800s she was known for kidnapping free black people and selling them as slaves. When Cannon was in her sixties, one of her tenants discovered a grave by accident when his plow horse sank into a hollow. He unearthed a blue chest, which he opened to find not a secret stash of cash but the corpse of a slave trader Cannon had killed years before for a large sum he had been carrying. The tenant went to the authorities, who, after many years of turning a blind eye to Cannon's depraved dealings, were forced to arrest her. The investigation of Cannon's property led to the discovery of several other bodies, some of which were children. Cannon's victims never received justice; rather than stand trial, Cannon poisoned herself in 1829 while in prison.

> **"MURDER IS TERRIBLY EXHAUSTING."** —ALBERT CAMUS

‹ PEOPLE EATER PACKER ›

Alfred Packer was the first man ever to be convicted for cannibalism under Colorado state law. In 1874 Packer and five other miners split from their party to seek silver in the San Juan Mountains. Sixty-five days later, Alfred Packer strolled back into town—alone. He also brandished a large cash roll as well as a gun that had belonged to one of the other miners. Packer was quickly jailed, only to escape. It didn't take long to locate the bodies of his former companions and confirm that Packer had killed and eaten the five miners. It took nine years to catch him, and another three to convict and sentence him to forty years in prison. Today he is gone but not forgotten: the University of Colorado at Boulder sports a memorial grill named after him, and one of the grill's most popular entrées is called the Packerburger.

⟨ FLORIDA'S FEMALE SERIAL KILLER ⟩

Aileen Wuornos had a textbook serial-killer childhood. Her father died in prison, and her fifteen-year-old mother abandoned her to her grandparents when she was an infant. Wuornos had a baby herself at the age of fourteen; when her grandmother passed away and her hard-drinking grandfather started beating her and her brother, she left home, taking to the road and supporting herself as a prostitute. Wuornos collected arrests for crimes such as driving drunk, assault, and passing bad checks, and she was known under a variety of different aliases.

Her rough-and-tumble life was briefly brightened when she met Tyria Moore, a hotel maid, at a gay bar in Daytona, Florida. The couple moved in together, and Wuornos supported them by turning tricks. Things started to fall apart in the late 1980s, when Moore's alcohol addiction got the best of her and Wuornos met Richard Mallory, a trash-talking ex-con man who picked her up off the highway. According to Wuornos, she was sitting in Mallory's car listening to him rant about women and rape and killing, and she "snapped," pulling out the .22-caliber gun she kept in her purse and shooting him three times. His body was found, decomposing, days later off the side of the highway.

After that incident, the bodies of several more men began cropping up around the same area. Meanwhile, Wuornos started bringing home extravagant trinkets, and Moore pretended not to wonder why her partner could suddenly pay the rent again.

The jig was finally up in June 1990, when Wuornos and Moore were found driving the car of a man who went missing days earlier. Florida police chased the women for several days and finally apprehended Wuornos in a bar. She was convicted of six counts of murder and sentenced to die, which she did, by lethal injection, in 2002.

"The consequences of our crimes long survive their commission, and, like the ghosts of the murdered, forever haunt the steps of the malefactor." —SIR WALTER SCOTT

⊰ DOCTOR DEATH ⊱

Not all doctors put their patients' health at the top of their list of priorities. Dr. Harold Shipman was one such physician—a British general practitioner who is said to have killed up to 250 of his patients in the 1990s. A friendly, well-liked doctor, Shipman had an easy way with his patients and had been practicing for many years. Nothing seemed out of the ordinary until a colleague, asked to cosign many of his cremation orders, noticed that his patients were dying in droves. She alerted the police, who, after some initial bungling, focused in on the death of Kathleen Grundy, an older woman who was found dead at her home in 1998. According to her will, Grundy had left all of her money—the sizable sum of more than 350,000 pounds—to Shipman, ignoring her children and grandchildren entirely. Police exhumed Grundy's body and found traces of diamorphine, or heroin, in her system. According to her family and friends, Grundy had never used a drug in her life.

Police seized Shipman's medical records and honed in on fifteen similar cases for investigation. A pattern emerged—Shipman would administer a lethal dose of heroin, sign the death certificate, and then alter the medical records to indicate the patient was in poor health. In some cases, he would manipulate his victims into leaving him money. The doctor was brought to trial and sentenced to fifteen consecutive life sentences for the fifteen murders, though it was estimated that he took part in as many as 250 deaths.

⟨ BLACK WIDOWS ⟩

"Black widow" is the slang term for women who use poison to kill their victims. People have used this silent but deadly method of murder for hundreds of years, but one of the better known black widows from modern times was Nannie Hazel Doss, also known as "the Giggling Grandma" for her sweetly nervous disposition. Over the course of thirty-four years, Doss killed eleven of her family members—including four husbands and two children—using arsenic.

5. COINCIDENCE OR SYNCHRONICITY?

ODD THINGS HAPPENING TO ORDINARY FOLKS

> **"COINCIDENCE IS GOD'S WAY OF REMAINING ANONYMOUS."**
> —ALBERT EINSTEIN

⟨ SOLE SURVIVORS ⟩

On December 5, 1664, the first event in the greatest series of coincidences in history occurred. On this date, a ship in the Menai Strait, off north Wales, sank with eighty-one passengers on board. There was one survivor—a man named Hugh Williams. On the same date in 1785, a ship sank in the Menai Strait with sixty passengers aboard. There was one survivor—a man named Hugh Williams. On the very same date in 1860 in exactly the same area, a ship sank with twenty-five passengers on board. There was one survivor—a man named Hugh Williams.

⟨ OUIJA MAGIC ⟩

A wealthy Connecticut woman named Helen Dow Peck believed messages she received from Ouija boards. One day in 1919, the board spelled out that she should leave her entire estate to a man named John Gale

Forbes. That she did—the only problem was that she didn't know anybody by that name. In fact, after she died in 1956, her lawyer did a search throughout the world and discovered that, despite what the all-knowing spirits had said, there was nobody with that name.

⟨ BROTHERLY FATE ⟩

In Bermuda, in 1975 and 1976, two brothers were killed in strikingly similar accidents. The first was riding a moped when he was struck and killed by a taxi. One year later, the man's brother, riding the same moped, was struck by the same taxi driver who had killed the first man, and the taxi was carrying the same passenger.

⟨ TWIN SHIPWRECKS ⟩

In 1922 the *Lyman Stewart* was wrecked off the coast of Lands End, San Francisco's rockiest and most treacherous section of coast. In 1937, the *Frank Buck* was wrecked on the exact same rock where the *Lyman Stewart* had gone down. The odd thing? Both ships were built as twin ships, side by side in the shipyard of their origin.

You can still see the ruins of the shipwrecks. If you visit Lands End, now part of the Golden Gate National Park Conservancy, take the stairs that lead from the Merrie Way parking lot and head onto the Coastal Trail between the Vista Point and the Palace of the Legion of Honor. At low tide you can often spot the *Lyman Stewart*'s steam engine and the *Frank Buck*'s stern post and steam engine sticking up out of the waters off the shore.

⟨ THE THREEFOLD LAW ⟩

In Louisville, Kentucky, three family members died in the same spot, on separate dates. A woman was hit by a car—an accident that she survived but that killed her six-week-old daughter. A few years later, the same woman was killed about two blocks away as she jumped from a moving vehicle for an undisclosed reason. But the cruel coincidence continued when twenty years later, the woman's nineteen-year-old son died on the same street when his motorcycle hit a car full of college students.

⟨ THE OL' SWITCHEROO ⟩

Irv Kupcinet experienced a rare kind of synchronicity while covering the coronation of Queen Elizabeth II in London in 1953. He found items in a hotel room drawer that were identified as those of Harry Hannin. Hannin, widely known as a Harlem Globetrotter, was actually a good friend of Kupcinet's. Just a few short days later, Kupcinet received a letter from Hannin. In the letter, Hannin explained that he had been in a hotel room in Paris and had found a tie in a drawer that had Kupcinet's name on it.

⟨ COINCIDENCE OR JUSTICE? ⟩

A man attempting to rob a convenience store in Cherryville, North Carolina, thwarted his own plans when he dropped the gun. The gun hit the ground, went off, and the bullet went into the robber's foot.

⟨ HEART ATTACK ⟩

In Rome, an Italian who was charged with killing his American girlfriend, after having kidnapped their daughter, died of a heart attack while testifying in court during his trial. Family members and friends claimed that he had threatened to kill her many times, and they were convinced he was guilty. Perhaps divine justice played a role in his eventual death.

⊰ A MESSAGE IN A BOTTLE ⊱

According to the *Journal Times* of Racine, Wisconsin, there is new evidence that destiny plays a role in love. On August 18, 2007, a young couple, Melody Kloska and Matt Behrs, tied the knot in a simple ceremony at the Wind Point Lighthouse in Racine. After the ceremony, they tossed a bottle containing their wedding vows into the cool blue waters of Lake Michigan.

Just a few weeks later, the newlyweds received a divine sign that they were meant-to-be. A letter arrived from Fred and Lynette Dubendorf, who had found the bottle while walking on a beach in Pentwater, Michigan, located on the other side of Lake Michigan. The letter explained that the Dubendorfs discovered the bottle on the very beach where they had been married twenty-eight years before. Not only that, but the Dubendorfs had been married on August 18, 1979.

⊰ A CHILD'S STORY ⊱

Anne Parrish, famed American novelist who wrote dozens of award-winning books from the 1920s through the 1950s, was one day browsing through books in a Parisian bookstore. She found a book that had always been a favorite of hers, *Jack Frost and Other Stories*. Delighted to find a memory from her childhood, she was shocked to discover that the inscription within contained her own name and the address of her childhood home in Colorado.

⟨ DOUBLE DEATH ⟩

In Germany in the late 1970s, a story hit all the newspapers, television and radio stations—a story that contained one of the most tragic examples of synchronicity to date. A man was walking along a country road at night when a car struck him from behind and killed him. One year from the day he died, the man's twin brother went for a walk at that same spot, in memory of his departed brother. As it turned out, the driver of the car that hit and killed the first man also had a twin brother. The driver's twin brother decided to drive along the same road, in memory of his own departed brother. He hit and killed the twin brother of the pedestrian, recreating a scene that has shocked everyone who has heard the story.

⟨ PAW PAW TRAGEDY ⟩

According to the *Detroit Free Press*, in February of 2007, in the Paw Paw Township, Michigan, two brothers were killed in a head-on collision with each other. The brothers, ages twenty-four and thirty-three, shared a home. The elder brother lost control of his vehicle and crossed into the path of his brother's oncoming car. They were both pronounced dead at the scene.

SYNCHRONIZE YOUR LIFE
▶➤ TOLD BY AMBER GUETEBIER ◀◀

In 2000, I traveled abroad for the first time and was happy to be visiting a friend who had recently moved to the beautiful city of Amsterdam, Netherlands. Upon arrival, the old friend met me, and we immediately began to wander the labyrinth of streets and canals. In the spirit of fun, we took several photos of ourselves, holding the camera up and capturing our own faces at funny angles.

After spending a few weeks in Amsterdam, I went on to travel to Ireland and Spain, returning to the Netherlands with a new beau in tow, just as spring was setting in. Happy to be back in the beautiful city, I started looking for under-the-table work. A local restaurant hired me, and I was befriended by a kooky Englishman who told me about a cheap "squat" I could stay in, for the grand fee of ten U.S. dollars a month. My boyfriend and I jumped at the chance and promptly moved into the building. It was a run-down, leaning brick row house, with a flooded basement and three creaking floors, no running toilet, and a mixture of travelers from around the world, including an eccentric Irish painter, an Israeli soldier, and the wild Englishman.

Once we had a bit of money saved, and we knew we would be around awhile, I decided to get my rolls of film from the earlier part of my trip developed. It was then that I realized the coincidence: the first photograph that my friend had taken of us shortly after my plane touched down was in front of the very building I had ended up living in! Not realizing it when I went to the squat for the first time, I had to see the photo to realize I had been in the exact place where I would later live.

⟨ DESTINED TO LOVE ⟩

This is the story of John and Martha O'Brien, originally told to Phil Cousineau for his book *Coincidence or Destiny?*:

THE BOOK OF THE BIZARRE

In 1989 a group of people from around the United States gathered in Paris to participate in a Bohemian Paris art and literary tour. On the third day of the tour, Martha Fletcher, a dancer from San Francisco, met John O'Brien, an artist from Greenwich Village, on a houseboat that rested on the Seine near the Pont d'Alma, in front of the Eiffel Tower. The two hit it off, but at the end of the tour they returned to their respective homes.

It wasn't until several months later, when Martha was moving into a new home that she realized that a photograph she had kept on her bulletin board since grade school was a painting of a houseboat on the Seine at Pont d'Alma, and the Eiffel Tower was in the background.

A few months later, John moved to San Francisco for the summer. With him, he brought a painting he had painted ten years before—of a ballerina with long red hair. The dancer looked exactly like Martha.

It was no surprise that the following summer the pair returned to Paris, John painting and Martha dancing. They spent a day in Moret sur Loing, a charming little village outside of Paris. At the end of the summer, however, they again parted, only this time John was returning to New York to move out to California permanently.

As he was packing his things he too came upon an old photo that he had kept for years. It was a photo of a painting of the little town of Moret sur Loing.

One year later, Martha and John married. One year after that, Martha was sorting through old boxes to make room for a nursery, and she happened upon a diary she had written when she was twelve. As she browsed through the pages, one line in particular stood out: "I wish I could be Michelle O'Brien." Michelle O'Brien was a ballet dancer that Martha had admired as a youth. Two months later, Martha gave birth to their daughter, Michelle O'Brien.

THE WARNING
▶ TOLD BY DENISE MURPHY BURKE ◀

Several years ago, I organized a Northwestern University reunion of my sorority sisters. We were all to stay at a sister's home in Santa Rosa, California. A group of about twenty of us were able to come, some from as far away as New York. I was immensely excited about the reunion and especially looking forward to the arrival of my best buddy, Barbara, from Ohio.

The afternoon prior to her arrival, I received a long-distance call from her. She said, "My suitcase is packed,

THE BOOK OF THE BIZARRE

and my ticket is in my hand, but I just don't think I can come."

It seems her son had called and begged her not to go. He had had a very powerful dream in which she was in a fatal accident at the reunion. My friend said that based on that alone she would have changed her plans. But her son had confessed to her that he had also had a similar dream three years before that his father would die very suddenly; five days after that dream his father died while taking a shower. His father was only forty-eight years old. The son felt somehow responsible for his dad's death, and due to his guilt had never shared the dream with his mom. But now he was desperate to convince her to stay home, and she did.

Even though Barbara wasn't with us, the first day was incredible. The plan for the second day was to take a horse-drawn, open-wagon ride through the vineyard countryside. That morning, nine of us climbed up on the first carriage as the driver was hoisting his large body into the driver's seat. Suddenly, the two horses mistook a loud sound for a signal to go. They lurched forward, throwing the driver on the ground. With no one to keep them in check, we were soon going at a full gallop!

I reached up to the driver's seat and pulled back on a large wooden lever, which seemed like it should be the brake. The lever did nothing to slow the wagon, but I held on to it for dear life. The others threatened to jump, but I begged them to hold tight.

We were racing out of control, and all of a sudden, we realized the freeway was straight ahead of us. The horses were heading right for it. But as the horses approached the freeway, they took a sudden ninety-degree turn on two wheels onto a frontage road. At full speed, the horses headed directly for one of the telephone poles that lined the road. The pole ended up going right between the two horses, smashing the yoke and freeing them. Everyone but I was violently flung out of the carriage. Women lay strewn on the ground like rag dolls. No one sustained serious injuries. But when the police arrived and asked me the names of the others, I couldn't answer. I just kept wondering, "What would have happened to Barbara if she had gone with us?"

I think that a deep connection between mother and son saved her life.

꒰꒰꒰

"In the magical universe there are no coincidences and there are no accidents. Nothing happens unless someone wills it to happen." —WILLIAM S. BURROUGHS

꒰꒰꒰

NIGHT OF TERROR

▬▬▶❭ TOLD BY JOANNE WARFIELD ❬◀▬▬

My throat ached with an excruciating pounding. It was my heart! It was so loud that I was sure I would be detected in my third hiding place in the shed. Who was this madman stalking me with a gun? What did he want from me?

Finally, catching my breath, I braved a peek around the corner of my shelter and decided to run for cover in the main house. I dashed through the clearing toward the house, slipped in through a side door, and slid the lock shut as quietly as possible.

I leaned back against the wall and slid down into a heap. Just as my heart began to slow down a bit, I heard a wild screeching of tires in the driveway. I rolled onto my knees and looked out the bottom of the window. Through a tear in the curtain, I could see the maniac in the driver's seat headed straight for the house at full speed.

I leapt to my feet and ran out the back door toward the orchard. In a flash I heard the car behind me. I turned the corner of the house, and the wheels screeched after me. My God, I thought, this was it—I was going to die!

Then I bolted upright in bed, stricken with terror. My heart was thundering in my chest and throat. It took me several minutes to realize that I was actually home and experiencing a nightmare! The fear lingered. I was so shaken by the experience that I made myself get up and walk around to stay awake. I turned on music and sang out loud to dispel the mood so there would be no chance of reentering what was a very real, frightening place. I knew this was no ordinary dream. It was 2 A.M., so I had some tea and, after an hour or so, somehow managed to get back to sleep.

Two days later, I was speaking with my mother, who lived several states away. She related to me a horrifying story about how she and my sister had been chased into hiding by my sister's crazy husband, who had threatened to shoot them. They frantically tried to find a place to hide. They hid in the shed, then in one of the cars, where they slept all night. They were truly terrified for their lives.

The incident had happened at 2 A.M. on the very night of my own nightmare.

⟨ PSYCHIC MADAME ⟩

No one can claim that Madame de Ferriem wasn't psychic. In 1896, the German medium had a premonition, which was published in the local papers, of a disastrous collapse of a coal mine in Dux, Bohemia. The following year, an accident in the exact mine killed hundreds of people.

> Both William Shakespeare and Miguel de Cervantes, who was considered by some to be Shakespeare's literary equivalent, died on the same day: April 23, 1616.

> In 1958, a Kansas tornado ripped a woman out of her house and deposited her, unharmed, sixty feet away, next to an LP of the song "Stormy Weather."

⟨ PSYCHIC WIFE ⟩

The wife of Ulysses S. Grant woke on April 14, 1865, with the intense sense that she and her husband should get out of Washington, D.C., as soon as possible. They left that day, even though it meant standing up President Abraham Lincoln's invitation to the theater. That's why Grant was not killed by John Wilkes Booth that evening when the actor assassinated the president. Booth's papers later revealed that Grant was on his hit list.

⟨ PRESCIENT LITERATURE ⟩

➤ In *Gulliver's Travels*, written in 1726, Jonathan Swift describes two moons revolving around Mars, in close proximity to the planet. One hundred and fifty-one years later, astronomers proved that Mars does indeed have two moons, and these moons are not far from the planet's surface.

➤ Author Morgan Robertson wrote his story of a gigantic luxury ship, the *Titan*, in 1898. In this fictional tale, the ship, advertised as unsinkable, hits an iceberg and tragically goes down, killing many passengers and crew. In 1912, the real-life ship the *Titanic* met its shockingly similar fate.

In 1914, Robertson wrote another novel about a future war involving fantastical weaponry called sunbombs, which were capable of decimating an entire city. In the book, the war starts in December and is brought on by the Japanese, who carry out a sneak attack on Hawaii.

⟨ LISTEN TO YOUR DREAMS ⟩

Countess Toutschokoff was the wife of a Russian general at the time that Napoleon was invading Moscow. During that time, she woke from a dream in which her father had come into her room with her young son and said that her husband had been killed at Borodino. The next two nights, she had the same dream. Finally she told her husband about it, and they looked at a map but could find no such town. Later that same year, her father came into her room early one morning, holding her son's hand and saying that her husband had indeed been killed at Borodino, a small town outside Moscow.

In *Paris in the Twentieth Century*, Jules Verne describes the Paris skyline dominated by a large metallic structure. The book was written in 1863, years before the Eiffel Tower was conceptualized in 1887.

FIRST IMPRESSIONS
▶▷ TOLD BY ANN B. IGOE ◁◀

Once my daughter and I went to the airport in Charleston, South Carolina, to pick up a woman and her son from South Africa. We had never seen her before, and I was not enthusiastic to be seeing her at this time. She was a woman that my husband had met on one of his trips. She had entertained him, and he had invited her to visit us if she ever came to America.

She was not difficult to recognize. She had the audacity to arrive wearing a khaki suit and pith helmet, and she walked about our little airport as though on a safari.

When she marched into our living room, she stopped dead in her tracks, gasped, and shouted for her son to come immediately. He found her standing in front of a painting that my daughter and I had bought in a small village in southern France.

He could not believe his eyes. He said, "This is the painting that my mother and I fell in love with in a small village in southern France, but because our funds were low, we had lunch to think about it before making our decision. When we returned to buy the painting, we were told that it had just been sold to an American woman and her daughter."

They had settled for a lesser painting by the same artist, and they just happened to have a photograph showing the painting hanging in their living room in South Africa.

Of course, new friendships were cemented on the spot.

⟨ MAYBE HE HAD A POINT ⟩

An agoraphobic man who had vowed never to leave the house again after he was assaulted at age eighteen decided, after thirty years of self-induced imprisonment, to take a walk outside. But the strain of being out was too much for him: he suffered a heart attack while strolling along.

"Whether we name divine presence synchronicity, serendipity, or graced moments matters little. What matters is the reality that our hearts have been understood. Nothing is as real as a healthy dose of magic which restores our spirits." —NANCY LONG

⟨ ONE HARDY BOOK ⟩

When British actor Anthony Hopkins signed up to play a leading role in the film *The Girl from Petrovka*, based on a book by George Feifer, he traveled to London to pick up a copy of the book for research. Although he visited many bookshops, he was unable to find a copy of the book anywhere. Waiting for a train at an underground station, Hopkins noticed a book sitting on a bench near him, apparently discarded. When he went to see what it was, he was amazed to find that it was *The Girl from Petrovka*, the very book he'd been searching for! As if this wasn't enough, years later while shooting the film, Hopkins was introduced to the book's author. The two men discussed the film and the book it was based on, and Feifer offhandedly mentioned that he didn't own a copy of the book himself anymore. He'd leant it to a friend who had lost it somewhere in London. Hopkins, incredulous, produced his found copy of the book, the margins of which were covered with the original owner's notes—made with Feifer's own hand.

> Novelist Ernest Hemingway and poet Hart Crane were both born on July 21, 1899. Both struggled with alcoholism and depression, and both committed suicide.

> A man was speeding down a highway at 110 mph when he struck the back of a car, immediately killing the two people inside. The victims? The man's mother and her elderly neighbor, whom she was taking on a leisurely drive to see the town's Christmas lights.

6. MORBID WRITERS AND TORTURED ARTISTS

FROM EDGAR ALLAN POE TO VINCENT VAN GOGH

‹ WAKING DREAMS ›

G. H. Lewis, the companion of novelist George Eliot, told the following story of Charles Dickens:

Dickens dreamt that he was in a room where everyone was dressed in scarlet. He stumbled against a lady standing with her back towards him. As he apologized, she turned her head and said, quite unprovoked, "My name is Napier."

He knew no one of the name Napier, and the face was unknown to him. Two days later, before he was to give a reading, a lady friend came into his waiting room accompanied by an unknown lady in a scarlet opera-cloak. The unknown woman, said his friend, "is very determined of being introduced."

"Not Miss Napier?" he jokingly inquired.

"Yes, Miss Napier."

Although the face of the woman Dickens had seen in his dream was not the face of the actual Miss Napier, the coincidence of the cloak and name was striking.

American author Norman Mailer once stabbed his wife and then wrote a novel about it (*An American Dream*).

⟨ THOU SHALT NOT STEAL? ⟩

The Bible is the number one book stolen in the United States, according to booksellers across America. Strange, seeing as people are giving out Bibles for free so often—and not to mention that the Bible's Ten Commandments forbid stealing.

> **"I DON'T USE DRUGS. MY DREAMS ARE FRIGHTENING ENOUGH."**
> —M. C. ESCHER

⟨ BAD SHOT ⟩

Despite being a self-avowed junkie and homosexual, William S. Burroughs (1914–1997) was a real lady-killer

—literally. One long night in Mexico, filled with booze and drugs, he tried to shoot a martini glass off the head of his common-law wife, Joan, with a pistol. He missed, hitting her in the forehead and killing her. Charged with involuntary manslaughter, he fled Mexico.

> Surrealist Salvador Dali owned an ocelot as a pet.
> Author Isabelle Allende always begins writing her next novel on January 8.

⟨ FRAMING YOUR HUSBAND ⟩

Agatha Christie nearly pulled off a real-life hoax worthy of her mystery novels. Upset that her husband was leaving her for another woman, she set up an incriminating scene that almost got him arrested for her "murder." Luckily for him, an employee at a distant seaside hotel saw news photos of Christie and recognized her as the woman who had slipped into the hotel under an assumed name. Although Christie claimed amnesia, the police were not amused after having wasted a week of searching rivers and bogs for her body.

‹ STRANGER THAN FICTION ›

This hoax is still accepted by many as genuine: *The Education of Little Tree* by Forrest Carter was purported to be the genuine memoir of a Cherokee orphan learning the ways of his tribe and nature while struggling to live in a white world. The book, still in print, turns out to have been written by a white supremacist and Ku Klux Klan member named Asa Carter.

Misha Defonseca's 1997 holocaust memoir, *Misha: A Memoire of the Holocaust Years*, attracted media attention in 2007 when a genealogical researcher found that the author had fabricated details about her life during World War II. The book, which was sold to its publisher as non fiction, tells a fascinating story of the author's travels through Europe following the execution of her parents by Nazis. The author, who represents herself as a Jew, kills a German soldier, is taken in by a pack of wolves, and wanders into the Warsaw Ghetto and escapes. After it was discovered that

Ms. Defonseca spent the war safely in Brussels (and that she was not even Jewish), she confessed: "There are times when I find it difficult to differentiate between reality and my inner world. The story in the book is mine. It is not actual reality—it was my reality." The "memoir" had been a best seller in Europe and Canada, and was the basis for a French film.

San Francisco's literary community was shocked to discover in 2006 that JT LeRoy, the purported 25-year-old HIV-positive former male prostitute, was in fact a 40-year-old woman named Laura Albert. LeRoy's first novel, *Sarah,* was published in 2000 to much critical acclaim. Supposedly based on LeRoy's life story, it told of the young man's experiences as a cross-dressing male prostitute in the deep South, a position that his drug-addled mother allegedly forced him into. LeRoy then escaped to San Francisco, where Laura Albert and her husband, Geoffrey Knoop, took him in.

LeRoy's remarkable story attracted the attention of literary celebrities, film directors, and even rock stars. He was encouraged to publish his short story collection, and his next book, *Labour,* was due out that spring. LeRoy was pathologically shy and showed up heavily disguised in his rare public appearances, often wearing dark sunglasses and refusing to speak. It was said that he appeared incognito at his own readings, at which members of the literary community would read for him because of his supposed stage fright. LeRoy's elusive nature only fueled the public's obsession with him.

On January 9, 2006, *The New York Times* revealed that JT LeRoy didn't exist—he was the grand creation of Albert, Knoop, and Knoop's half-sister Savannah, who had made his public appearances in heavy disguise. Albert had written the novels and stories and had conducted LeRoy's first phone interviews using a West Virginia accent. What's more, the couple had fabricated the identities of LeRoy's supposed street friend, Speedie, and Emily Frasier, another woman he had lived with. The elaborate hoax was reportedly a way for Knoop and Albert, whose rock band Thistle was marginally popular in the San Francisco music scene, to gain access to rich and famous circles and promote their band.

"The lightning flashes through my skull; mine eyeballs ache and ache; my whole beaten brain seems as beheaded, and rolling on some stunning ground."

—HERMAN MELVILLE

DON'T BELIEVE EVERYTHING YOU READ: "PETRIFIED MAN FOUND IN NEVADA CAVE"

➤ FROM THE VIRGINIA CITY *TERRITORIAL ENTERPRISE*, 1862 ◄

The story: According to the article, a petrified man with a wooden leg was found in a cave in a remote part of Nevada. The man was found in a seated position, with "the right thumb resting against the side of his nose, the left thumb partially supported the chin, the forefinger pressing the inner corner of the left eye and drawing it partially open; the right eye was closed, and the fingers of the right hand spread apart." The article claimed the man had been dead for at least 300 years.

The reaction: The story spread to other newspapers in Nevada, then to the rest of the country, and then around the world. The archaeological "find" was even reported in the London scientific journal *Lancet*.

The truth: The story was the work of the *Territorial Enterprise*'s local editor, Samuel Clemens (later known by his pen name, Mark Twain). Clemens figured people would know it was a hoax by the description of the petrified man's hand positions. (Try doing it yourself.) But he was wrong.

⟨ BUNNY LOVER ⟩

American children's author Margaret Wise Brown (1910–1952), who wrote many a tender kitty-and-bunny tale, including *Goodnight Moon* and *The Bunny's Birthday*, loved to hunt rabbits. She collected their severed feet as trophies.

> "WRITING IS EASY: ALL YOU DO IS SIT STARING AT A BLANK SHEET OF PAPER UNTIL DROPS OF BLOOD FORM ON YOUR FOREHEAD." —GENE FOWLER

⟨ OBSESSED WITH WHITMAN ⟩

When American poet Walt Whitman died in 1892, his brain was put in a jar and donated to the University of Pennsylvania. The university doesn't have it any more—a lab technician dropped the jar on the floor and damaged the brain. The university quietly discarded it, and Whitman's "Specimen Days" were over.

⟨ STRANGE SYNCHRONICITY ⟩

Mark Twain was born in 1835, a year when Haley's comet could be seen from earth, and, fulfilling his own prophecy, he died in 1910, the next time the comet cycled near the earth, seventy-six years later.

The Museum of Modern Art in New York City hung Henri Matisse's *Le Bateau* upside down for forty-seven days before an art student noticed the error.

⟨ FLUNKIES ⟩

Novelist Edgar Allen Poe, painter James Whistler, and mind traveler Timothy Leary were all once students at the U.S. Military Academy at West Point. Not surprisingly, none of them made it through to graduation or to an officership in the military. Poe flunked out in a particularly spectacular way. An order came for cadets to show up for a full-dress parade wearing "white belt and gloves, under arms." He followed the order all too literally, appearing wearing nothing but a belt and carrying his gloves under his naked arms.

‹ DA VINCI CODE ›

Leonardo Da Vinci was a notoriously secretive man. He kept clandestine notes to himself in a distinct style: he wrote backwards, from right to left. Turns out Da Vinci's code wasn't too hard to crack: it was easily legible when held up to a mirror.

➤ German composer Richard Wagner planned to be buried in a grave in his garden and was known to divulge this fact willingly to dinner party guests. He would take them to view the garden and then delight in the reactions of his guests as they sat back down to finish the meal. Wagner and his wife, Cosima, were indeed buried in the Bayreuth, Germany garden.

➤ Poet Ezra Pound wrote *The Pisan Cantos* while imprisoned at a U.S. Army camp in Pisa, Italy. He had been arrested for treason because he had broadcast Fascist propaganda from Italy during World War II. Eventually judged insane, Pound spent twelve years in a Washington, D.C., mental hospital before returning to Italy.

≺ STOP AND SMELL (OR DON'T) ≻

Voltaire always fainted whenever he smelled roses. He also drank seventy cups of coffee a day. Are the two facts related?

"I am not strictly speaking mad, for my mind is absolutely normal in the intervals, and even more so than before. But during the attacks it is terrible—and then I lose consciousness of everything. But that spurs me on to work and to seriousness, as a miner who is always in danger makes haste in what he does." —VINCENT VAN GOGH

≺ POETIC CALENDAR ≻

If you want to be poet laureate of the United States, it might help if you were born on March 1. Three previous laureates were born on that date—Howard Nemerov, Richard Wilbur, and Robert Hass.

⟨ WORKS BEST UNDER THE INFLUENCE ⟩

Robert Louis Stevenson (1850–1894) wrote *Dr. Jekyll and Mr. Hyde*, a tome of 60,000 words, during a six-day cocaine binge. He was also reported to have been suffering from tuberculosis at the time.

LEO TOLSTOY'S LIBRARY AND MANUSCRIPTS WERE DESTROYED BY A MOB OF PEASANTS IN 1917.

⟨ ART WAS HIS FALLBACK ⟩

Besides being a master stonecutter and painter, Michelangelo was an up-and-coming author. He carved his statue of David whilst waiting for his editor to approve his novel, a thriller called *Chislers in Florence*.

English poet Percy Bysshe Shelley (1792–1822) suffered from recurring hallucinations of a deranged gunman stalking him.

- French playwright Moliere (1622–1673) was playing the lead role in his play *The Hypochondriac* when he collapsed into fits of coughing and hemorrhaging onstage. He was suffering from pulmonary tuberculosis and died hours later, at home.

- American playwright Tennessee Williams died when he choked to death on the plastic top of his nasal spray while alone in a hotel room in 1983.

- Percy Bysshe Shelley, romantic poet and husband of Mary Shelley, drowned in 1822 while sailing in his schooner, *Don Juan*, during a sudden storm. Days before, he had claimed to have met his doppelganger, who foretold his death. Mary, devastated, snatched her husband's heart from the funeral pyre and kept it for the rest of her life.

⟨ THE DEVIL MADE ME WRITE IT ⟩

Among the notable literary figures who counted themselves members of the Order of the Golden Dawn are Algernon Blackwood, Bram Stoker, and William Butler Yeats. Yeats's magical name was Daemon est Deus Inversus, which is Latin for "the devil is God backwards."

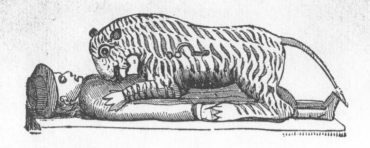

✦ BIZARRE LITERARY DEATHS ✦

➤ Sherwood Anderson (1876–1941), author of *Winesburg, Ohio*, died from complications from peritonitis, which he contracted after choking on a toothpick.

➤ British writers Aldous Huxley and C. S. Lewis both died on November 22, 1963, the day of John F. Kennedy's assassination.

➤ German poet Rainer Maria Rilke died of leukemia in 1926. Refusing to acknowledge the nature of his illness, Rilke believed he would die of blood poisoning after being pricked by a rose thorn. He even wrote his epitaph to that effect:

> *Rose, oh pure contradiction, joy*
> *of being No-one's sleep,*
> *under so many lids.*

> "GERTRUDE STEIN WAS A MASTER AT MAKING NOTHING HAPPEN VERY SLOWLY." —CLIFTON FADIMAN

⟨ WHERE'S VOLTAIRE? ⟩

Voltaire, author of countless satires—especially concerning the religious sector—was not well liked among people of faith. When he died in 1778, he was denied burial in church ground until 1791, when the abbey in Champagne relented and moved his remains to the Pantheon in Paris. But the late author did not rest in peace there, either. In 1814 a group of right-wing religious extremists broke into the Pantheon, exhumed his remains, and dumped them in a garbage heap somewhere. The heist was not discovered until fifty years later, when authorities found his sarcophagus empty.

⟨ THE MYSTERIOUS DEATH OF BITTER BIERCE ⟩

Ambrose Bierce was a prolific journalist and author whose biting cynicism earned him the nickname of Bitter Bierce. Perhaps the most interesting part of this literary dynamo's biography is his death—or, more accurately, his disappearance. Nobody knows exactly how or when Bierce died.

In October of 1913, Bierce departed his native Washington, D.C., to tour old Civil War battlefields in the Deep South, a trip he had been planning for some time. He passed through Louisiana and Texas, and by December he was in Mexico, at which point he promptly disappeared. The Mexican Revolution was in full swing, and according to some theories, Bierce met up with rebel leader Pancho Villa, who later executed him. Others place him on the front lines of the war, killed in battle. Bierce's daughter, alarmed by her elderly father's disappearance, petitioned the U.S. government to send out a search party for him, but the group found no conclusive evidence about what happened to him.

LITERARY DEATHMATCH
►❯ TURGENEV VS. DOSTOYEVSKY ❮◄

Ivan Sergeyevich Turgenev (1818–1883) once called fellow Russian novelist Fyodor Dostoyevsky (1821–1881) a "pimple on the face of literature."

- When writer, anthropologist, and folklorist Zora Neale Hurston died in 1960, she was buried in an unmarked grave in the Garden of Heavenly Rest in Fort Pierce, Florida—a cemetery designated for "Negros only." In 1973, author Alice Walker found her grave and had a gravestone erected in Hurston's honor.

- Pulitzer Prize–winning novelist Ellen Glasgow (1873–1945) requested that upon her death her two dogs be removed from their graves in her garden and be buried with her. They were.

- Poet Emily Dickinson's (1830–1886) final requests were that she would be buried in a white casket; that heliotropes be placed inside, along with a posy of blue violets placed at her throat; and that a wreath of blue violets be placed on top of the casket.

- Carson McCullers (1917–1967) suffered a series of debilitating strokes when she was in her twenties, which caused her to lose sight in her right eye. This malady seriously affected her productivity—she had to reduce her writing output to one page a day.

⟨ PARKER VS. LUCE ⟩

Twentieth-century American writers Dorothy Parker and Clare Boothe Luce never got along. Once, when Luce encountered Parker in a doorway, she stepped aside and remarked, "Age before beauty." Always quick with a comeback, Parker countered, "Pearls before swine," as she elegantly passed through.

After meeting Lord Byron at a ball, Lady Caroline Lamb wrote in her diary that the English poet was "mad, bad, and dangerous to know." But that didn't prevent the married Lady Lamb from entering into a scandalous and well-publicized affair with him.

7. DIA DE LOS MUERTOS

CORPSES ON CAMPUS, VOICES FROM BEYOND THE GRAVE,
STRANGE CEMETERY FACTS, SPOOKY SPECTERS,
AND OTHER GHOSTLY, GHASTLY, AND GOTHIC GOINGS ON

⟨ PREMATURE BURIAL ⟩

Lurid stories from the seventeenth and eighteenth centuries were spread in the popular press about premature burial. Some of these tales were spread by well-meaning doctors; for example, postmortem reports described corpses with their fingers chewed off—a sign, some doctors said, that the corpse awoke and was panicked and hungry enough to chew its own extremities. In reality, most or all of the cases were actually the result of rodent infestation.

However, there was good reason for people to be terrified of being buried alive. Physicians and medical professionals were not all particularly skilled at telling the difference between dead and unconscious, and burials happened so fast (due to the heat in some places and the absence of preserving chemicals) that it was not unheard of for a person to wake up underground.

John Bateson was an inventor with a paranoia about this very situation, and so he came up with the Bateson Revival Device—a small church bell attached to the lid of the coffin and connected to a cord strapped to the deceased's hand. The idea was if you woke up in a coffin, you could ring the bell until somebody rescued you. Because his fears were shared by hundreds of people, Bateson was made wealthy with the device.

⟨ DINING WITH THE DEAD ⟩

The New Lucky Restaurant in Ahmandabad, India, sits atop a centuries-old Muslim cemetery. For more than four decades, patrons have been able to dine at tables that are nestled between the graves, which resemble small cement coffins. Waiters maneuver through the cemetery with their trays of steaming food and milky tea, balancing between the tables and the graves. The unusual setting attracts customers from around the world, and the owners believe dining there brings good luck.

⟨ TINY TOMBSTONE ⟩

According to *Ripley's Believe It or Not*, the world's smallest tombstone is in Bates County, Missouri, and belongs to the gravesite of one Linnie Crouch. It is 4³/₈" x 3¹/₄" x 2¹/₂" thick.

⟨ RISING FROM THE GRAVE ⟩

In his book *Scottish Bodysnatchers: True Accounts*, author Norman Adams paints several gruesome tales of premature burial and inadvertent rescue. Among them is the account of Maggie Dickson, who was hung in 1724 in Inveresk, presumably for a self-induced abortion that she had attempted to conceal. Maggie was hung in the town square, and it is said that the hangman pulled and swung on her legs once the noose was tightened and the ladder was kicked out, just for good measure. She was cut down, apparently dead, and her body was put in a cart by her relatives to be taken home for burial. Along the way, the family and friends of the deceased Maggie stopped for a drink. While the mourners were inside the alehouse, Maggie regained consciousness. Her weak cries attracted help, and she was revived by a local surgeon. Later, she was granted her freedom and went on to live many years, being widely known as "Half-Hangit" Maggie.

A similar tale is one from Aberdeenshire, where Merjorie Elphinstone was buried alive and rousted from her premature eternal slumber by a grave robber who was trying to steal the rings from her fingers. And there is the story of the minister's wife, Margaret Halcrow. She was saved from an untimely fate when a sexton attempted to rob her grave and found her alive. Her husband was quite shocked to find her knocking on the door one evening.

HAUNTED CEMETERIES
⟨ ACROSS THE UNITED STATES ⟩

There are endless accounts of ghost sightings in the most logical of places: graveyards. Here are but a few of the most haunted cemeteries in the United States:

> THE MYRTLE HILL CEMETERY in Valley City, Ohio. This cemetery is known to be haunted by a witch, whose grave is marked by a heavy sphere.

> STULL CEMETERY in Kansas City, Kansas. Some refer to this cemetery, perhaps one of the most fantastical of all haunted cemeteries, as the Gates of Hell, the Cemetery of the Damned, and the Seventh Gate

to Hell. The devil himself is said to roam amongst the tombs. The devil's child is also said to dwell here, along with a boy who can change himself into a werewolf, and the ghost of a witch.

➤ CAMP CHASE CONFEDERATE CEMETERY in Columbus, Ohio. This cemetery is said to be haunted by a lady in gray.

➤ MASONIC CEMETERY in Central City, Colorado. Reputed to be haunted by the ghost of a woman who lays flowers on the grave of John Edward Cameron. She is said to appear on April 5 and November 1 and has been witnessed by entire groups of people.

➤ FOREST PARK CEMETERY in Brunswick, New York. Many phantoms are said to roam the headstones here, including ones that cause statues to bleed.

➤ ADELAIDA CEMETERY in Paso Robles, California. An evil poltergeist presence has been reported by both visitors and investigators. A ghost of a woman in a long white nightgown has been spotted by more than one visitor, usually between 10 P.M. and midnight on Fridays.

➤ ST. LOUIS CEMETERY in New Orleans, Louisiana. This graveyard is arguably one of the most haunted in all of North America. It is said to be home to multiple ghosts, including the famous Voodoo queen,

Marie Laveau. Visitors have reported hearing weeping and groaning and seeing mists and various other phenomena.

- WHITE CEMETERY in Barrington, Illinois. Witnesses report seeing eerie globes of light floating around the cemetery. Phantom images of a house and a car have also been seen nearby.

- MCCONNIO CEMETERY in Evergreen, Alabama. This cemetery is reputed to be haunted by soldiers of the Civil War.

- WESTERN BURIAL GROUND of the churchyard of Westminster Presbyterian Church in Baltimore, Maryland. This cemetery is the eternal resting place of Edgar Allan Poe and Francis Scott Key, among other famous people. Some visitors report sightings of the ghost of Poe himself. Other ghostly figures include those of a crazed lunatic and a drunken ghoul.

- LAKE FOREST CEMETERY in Grand Haven, Michigan. Sightings of spooky specters here include a pale bluish male, orbs, mists, black shadows, and the occasional disembodied voice.

"A COFFIN NAIL" IS SLANG FOR A CIGARETTE.

⟨ STAR LIFE ⟩

On April 21, 1997, a rocket containing the cremated remains of twenty-four people was launched into space. Among the remains were those of Gene Roddenberry, *Star Trek* series creator. The rocket was launched by Celestis, a company that formed in 1996 for the purpose of launching ashes into space.

> **"I AM TOLD HE MAKES A VERY HANDSOME CORPSE, AND BECOMES HIS COFFIN PRODIGIOUSLY."** —OLIVER GOLDSMITH

⟨ A TISKET, A TASKET ⟩

The words "coffin" and "casket" are commonly substituted for one another, but they do technically mean different things. A coffin is defined as a box or chest for burying a corpse and is generally wedge-shaped and simple. A casket is almost always rectangular and fancier than a coffin. In the fifteenth century, a casket was used to store jewels.

⟨ GOOD NIGHT AND GOOD LUCK ⟩

Ready to move on after a painful divorce? Then you should probably purchase a Wedding Ring Coffin. Described on the creators' Web site as "the perfect gift for yourself or a loved one for bringing closure after a divorce," the coffin allows you to "bury the past and move on to a new tomorrow."

Prices starting around $30 for beautiful miniature mahogany coffins inscribed with sayings such as, "Gone and forgotten," "Six feet isn't deep enough," and "I do NOT!"

Visit the company's Web site: *www.weddingringcofffin.com.*

Kutna Hora in the Czech Republic is home to an ossuary, a depository for bones of the dead. The Kutna Hora ossuary includes a chandelier that is reputed to contain every bone in the human body.

⟨ CEMETERY ICONOGRAPHY ⟩

In his book *Stories in Stone: A Field Guide to Cemetery Symbolism and Iconography,* author and photographer

Douglas Keister has compiled a reference guide for cemetery-goers that is equivalent to an Audubon field guide for ornithologists. Covering everything from Freemasonry symbols to the meanings of flowers, *Stories in Stone* is a must-have for any graveyard groupie. Keister teaches the reader that morning glories symbolize the resurrection, a draped urn may signify the veil between the earth and heavens, and a feather can represent ascent into heaven.

Some other common cemetery symbolism:

- An anchor is both a symbol of hope and the mark of a seafarer.
- Flowers represent love, beauty, and a brief life. Chrysanthemums are symbolic of longevity and immortality, calla lilies mean beauty and marriage, daisies often mark children's graves, and violets mean humility.
- A weeping willow expresses the sorrow of the deceased's surviving friends and family.
- A shaft of wheat generally means a long and abundant life.
- An acorn represents prosperity.

 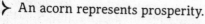

⟨ DEATHLY TRADITIONS ⟩

▶▶ DIA DE LOS MUERTOS OR NOCHE DE MUERTOS ◀◀

In Mexico, candles—one for each deceased relative—are lit by families on the night following November 1, *Dia de los Muertos* or Day of the Dead. November 1 is the day to honor dead children and wayward spirits, and November 2 is the day to honor deceased family members and friends. Families begin preparations sometimes weeks in advance. Arriving at the cemetery, they clean the graves and lay fresh soil to create the mounds of earth on which flowers, flower petals, and candles will be arranged in artful designs. Offerings are placed on the graves, including *pan de muerto* (bread for the dead), flowers, sugar skulls or sugar animals, and favorite items of the deceased. Each region has its own specific variations on the holiday. Some have lively processions with dancing, and people paint their faces to look like skeletons. Other areas' celebrations are more somber and include traditional songs and candlelit processions beginning at 12:01 A.M. on November 2.

▶▶ CHING MING OR GRAVE SWEEPING DAY ◀◀

Observed on April 5, this traditional day to honor the dead is celebrated by Chinese populations throughout the world. This annual celebration begins by weeding gravesites and cleaning headstones. Fresh flowers are brought to the graves, and incense and paper money are burned there. Some families bring also paper clothing or other items to burn as offerings.

Feasts are laid out on each of the graves as offerings to the ancestral spirits. Three sets of chopsticks and three Chinese wine cups are laid out next to each headstone. The head of the household bows three times with each wine cup, pouring its contents into the grave. Some families eat the feast on the graves as a kind of picnic, and others set off firecrackers to scare off evil spirits and let the dead know the living are there.

Especially in China, people carry willow branches with them and hang the branches on the front door of their houses to ward off any wayward or evil spirits that wander during the Ching Ming celebration.

≺ NEAR-DEATH EXPERIENCES ≻

"Near-death experience" was a term first coined by Raymond Moody, an American psychologist, in the 1970s. According to Moody, the following are characteristic phases of a near-death experience (NDE):

- First, people floated out of their bodies, leaving pain or injury behind. They were able to see things they could not have seen from the vantage point of their body. Many also reported being joined by guardian spirits and meeting dead relatives and friends.
- The next phase was a transitory one; people often compared it to floating along a passageway such as a tunnel or bridge.
- The NDE climaxed with a sensation of unconditional love or the feeling of coming home.
- A life review completed the experience.

⟨ HAUNTING LADIES ⟩

In the sixteenth century, Lady Glamis, convicted of witchcraft and trying to murder the king of Scotland, was burned at the stake. Her ghost now haunts Glamis Castle in Angus, Scotland. Many visitors have seen her floating above the clock tower. Meanwhile, Anne Boleyn, Catherine Howard, and Jane Seymour are all said to haunt Hampton Court Palace, just outside of London.

⊰ MORBID STUDENT BODIES ⊱

The students at the University of Colorado at Boulder are known for their morbid fascination with the local story of Alferd Packer and his cannibal monstrosities of the 1870s. Fifty years after Packer's conviction, the university students voted to rename the school cafeteria as the Alferd Packer Memorial Grill. It serves the usual standards, although some have unusual names. One of the most popular dishes is the "El Canibal" burrito.

⊰ THE BURTON AGNES SKULL ⊱

In 1598, the Griffin family decided to build a new home on their lands in Yorkshire. The three Griffin daughters were quite interested in the project, Anne in particular. Anne paid great attention to the construction of the Burton Agnes Hall from start to finish, and she was quite attached to the old house by the end.

One night, Anne was walking home on a road and was suddenly attacked by a gang of thieves. They struck her on the head, and if she had not been rescued by the villagers who had heard her screams, she most likely would have died immediately. She was quickly brought home to her family, but things did not look good. Before dying, Anne begged her sisters to keep a part of her in the Burton Agnes Hall forever. She decided, upon her final goodbye, that they should bury her skull within the walls of the house that she helped to build.

Anne died five days after she had been attacked, and her sisters ignored her request. Instead, they buried her, in one piece, in the church graveyard. Soon after the burial, the Griffin family heard bloodcurdling screams ringing out in Burton Agnes Hall, and no one could discover their source. Chilled to the bone, the sisters feared that the screams were a call from Anne to fulfill her dying wish. With no other solution in mind, the Griffin family decided that they must obey Anne's wishes and dig up her body immediately. When the coffin was opened, they received another terrible shock—the body had not decayed, but the head had fallen off and lost every bit of hair and tissue, leaving only a bare skull. The Griffins took Anne's skull home, and the screams subsided.

Everything was fine for many years after that, until the house was sold to another family who banished the skull from the Burton Agnes Hall. The screams promptly returned, and the horrified new inhabitants returned the skull to its place. The screams stopped yet again.

Later, a new owner moved in, hid the skull away within a wall, and never told anyone where it was. No one has found the skull since, and yet the screams have not returned. Some people claim to have seen Anne floating around the house in October, the month in which she was killed, perhaps searching for her own skull. They can recognize the ghost as Anne because it matches her portrait, which still hangs in the house to this very day.

⊰ JUNG AND HIS PATIENT ⊱

One night, after returning home from a lecture he had given, Carl Jung lay awake in bed for a long time. At about two o'clock, he had just fallen asleep, when he awoke with a start and had the feeling that someone had come into the room. He even thought that the door had been hastily opened. He turned on the light, but there was no one there. The room was still and quiet. He even leapt from his bed to check the corridor, which was also eerily quiet. He tried to recall exactly what had happened and why he had the urgent feeling that someone had come into the room. It suddenly occurred to him that he had been awakened by a feeling of dull pain, as though something had struck him in the fore-head and then the back of skull.

The following day, Jung received a telegram telling him that one of his patients had committed suicide. The man had shot himself in the head; the bullet had gone through his forehead and come to rest in the back wall of his skull.

In January 2008, the Dukinfield Crematorium in Manchester, England, asked local residents and clergymen to support its plan for heating and powering its chapel and boiler using the heat created by burning bodies.

⟨ MESSY MESSAGE ⟩

Are you prone to slovenly ways when dining? Food always falling off your fork and dropping onto your clothes? This may be a message from beyond. Judika Illes, known psychic and witch, tells us that this action can be a result of your ancestors trying to get your attention. She recommends setting up communication with them and then seeing if your table manners improve!

- Ancient Mesopotamians buried their deceased infants in large kitchen jars.
- In the ancient city of Jericho, the dead were buried under the houses they had lived in. But first their heads were severed, covered with plaster and clay, and decorated for their families to worship.

⤏ EVERLASTING GREEN ⤎

The Ecopod is a 100 percent biodegradable coffin, made from paper, untreated plywood, and fair-trade bamboo or handwoven willow. The Natural Burial Comany makes these eco-conscious vessels for the afterlife in a variety of colors, linings, and styles.

⤏ WAKE UP ⤎

In January of 2008, an eighty-one-year-old Chilean man woke up at his own funeral. His family dressed him in his finest suit and laid him out for a proper wake, only to witness him opening his eyes mid-mourning. Upon waking he simply asked for a glass of water. The family was overjoyed.

⟨ CORPSES ON CAMPUS ⟩

In the eighteenth and nineteenth centuries, medical schools in the United States used to routinely get their cadavers for dissection by grave robbing; faculty members and students themselves made midnight raids on local graveyards. It became the custom among grieving survivors in university towns to place iron bars on new graves and hire armed guards for two weeks until the body had time to putrefy enough to make it unusable for research. Between 1752 and 1852, there were at least thirteen riots by citizens against grave-robbing medical schools, including one in 1788 in New York City that killed eight people and injured scores of others.

⟨ HAUNTED CAMPUSES ACROSS THE U.S.A. ⟩

- University of Washington, Seattle: The College Inn Pub is haunted by a centuries-old murder victim.
- Yale University, New Haven, Connecticut: Woolsey Hall has hosted more than a dozen phantom concerts near its old organ.
- University of California, Berkeley: The school's Sather Tower is haunted by the ghost of a student who leapt from the tower in the 1960s.

➤ University of the South, Sewanee, Tennessee: Students over the years have reported a horrifying headless apparition at various locations across the campus. The ghost is seen in a traditional gown and is believed to be the spirit of a student who wore such a gown and was decapitated in a car accident.

⟨ ZOMBIE WALK ⟩

Do you like to walk with the dead? Prefer the moans of animated corpses to conversations with mortals? Well, you should probably join or organize a Zombie Walk. A Zombie Walk or Zombie March is an organized public gathering of two or more people who dress as zombies and wander around, limping their way in an organized route to a public center or cemetery. What a stress reliever!

⟨ RUN TO THE LIGHT, CAROL ANNE! ⟩

Poltergeists—noisy, active ghosts with the ability to control matter—were originally thought to be mischievous spirits. More modern beliefs target troubled teens as the source of alleged poltergeist activities; many psychics believe activity attributed to poltergeists is actually caused by adolescents unwittingly performing psychokinesis. Signs of poltergeist haunt-ings include:

➤ Objects being thrown about,
➤ Knockings, tappings, and rappings of unknown ori-gins and generally very disruptive,
➤ An adolescent or teenager living in the home and experiencing emotional turmoil,
➤ Paranormal activity that stops when the teen is absent,
➤ Apparitions that are not usually seen.

> "THERE ARE WRONGS WHICH EVEN THE GRAVE DOES NOT BURY."
> —HARRIET ANN JACOBS

⟨ VENETIAN FAIRIES ⟩

Spirits who dress in white and appear most often during the enchanting Venetian nights are said to be the *fade*, or fairies. They are thought to be the spirits of women who died in childbirth. They appear to be beautiful young ladies but are in fact treacherous. They have deformed feet—sometimes goat feet.

8. SYMPATHY FOR THE DEVIL

STRANGE ROCK-AND-ROLL STORIES

⊰ SECRET SPOOKY MESSAGES ⊱

Backmasking, an audio technique in which sounds are recorded backwards onto a track that is meant to be played forwards, is a deliberate process. Backward messaging is similar, but it may be unintentional. Backmasking has been a source of much controversy, especially related to the supposed subliminal messages it may provide. Many musicians have been reported to use backmasking in their records, and several of them have quite possibly *intentionally* included secret messages in their music when played backwards. You be the judge.

➤ LED ZEPPELIN, "STAIRWAY TO HEAVEN" ◄

Original lyrics: "If there's a bustle in your hedgerow, don't be alarmed now. It's just a spring clean for the May queen. Yes, there are two paths you can go by, but in the long run, there's still time to change the road you're on."

Played backwards: "Oh, here's to my sweet Satan. The one whose little path would make me sad, whose power is Satan. He'll give those with him 666, there was a little tool shed where he made us suffer, sad Satan."

Original lyrics: While played forward, there is a segment that may sound like indistinguishable gibberish.

Played backwards: The same segment is quite alarming when played backwards. What comes out rather clearly is, "Paul is a dead man. Miss him, miss him, miss him."

❮ SATAN LOVES HEAVY METAL ❯

Satanic messages are alleged to be found throughout heavy-metal music. Slayer's 1985 album *Hell Awaits* is a prominent example of hidden satanic messages in music. The album starts with a demonic-sounding voice that, when played backwards, urges listeners to "join us" over and over at increasing volumes.

The Cradle of Filth song "Dinner at Deviants Palace" consists almost entirely of ambient sounds and a reversed reading of the Lord's Prayer. (In the Middle Ages, being able to say the Lord's Prayer backwards was thought to be a sign that someone was a witch.)

Another lesser-known example is in the Alan Parsons Project album *The Turn of a Friendly Card*: at the very end of the first track, "May Be a Price to Pay," a backward message is inserted. Played forward, the English words are, "Something's been going on, there may be a price to pay." Played in reverse, the message, in clear Spanish, is, "*Escucha*, baby, *al Demonio, es bien fácil*" (Listen, baby, to the demon, it's so easy).

THE INTERNATIONAL
‹ STRANGE MUSIC FESTIVAL ›

In Olive Hill, Kentucky, the International Strange Music Festival was founded to honor people who make music from nonmusical items. Performers have included a Japanese trio playing "My Old Kentucky Home" on a table (upside down, strung like a cello), a teapot (a wind instrument), and assorted pots and pans (bongo drums). Other sets of performers were a fifteen-piece orchestra of automobile horns, a seven-foot slide whistle requiring three people to operate it, and a "graduated clanger"—a system of ever-smaller fire-alarm bells, played like a xylophone.

Four men dressed like Elvis jumped out of a plane to promote a Boston nightclub in 1996. Three of them lived, but one unlucky Elvis died when he caught a gust of wind and was blown out to sea.

⟨ TRULY ODD ⟩

Rock 'n' roller Gene Simmons, of the seventies group KISS, was once a high school teacher. He taught at a public school in Spanish Harlem while moonlighting on his music career. His tenure at Public School 75 was somewhat tenuous. He broke ranks with traditional English curriculum by using *Spiderman* comic books as teaching aids instead of classic Western literature. Years before, Simmons wrote a college English term paper titled, "The Social Significance of the Panel Graphic Art Form," devoted to the impact of comic strips on American culture.

> **"WE WANTED TO LOOK LIKE WE CRAWLED OUT FROM UNDER A ROCK IN HELL."** —GENE SIMMONS, ON THE AESTHETIC OF THE BAND KISS

⟨ NEVER COULD RESIST A PHOTO OP ⟩

In 1995, the three remaining Beatles, Paul McCartney, Ringo Starr, and George Harrison, went into the studio to add their voices to an old recording of "Free as a Bird" by their fallen bandmate, John Lennon. When they were finished, the three stars posed for a quick photo outside the studio. At the same moment that the shutter clicked, a white peacock ambled into the shot. McCartney was convinced that the bird was his friend John Lennon, reincarnated.

"It rubs me the wrong way, a camera . . . It's a frightening thing . . . Cameras make ghosts out of people."
—BOB DYLAN

⟨ WILL NOT LEAVE THE BUILDING ⟩

Elvis Presley recorded his 1956 hit song "Heartbreak Hotel" in RCA's broken down corporate headquarters and recording studio in Nashville, Tennessee. When the company finally moved out of the building, it was stripped and converted into a TV production facility that included an audio studio in the space where Elvis had recorded. Crew members at the renovated facility swore that every time the late star's name was mentioned in that space, something weird would happen—a lightbulb would burst, a ladder would fall, or the sound system would go haywire.

⟨ OCCULT PURIST ⟩

Before Led Zeppelin really took off, guitarist Jimmy Page owned and ran an occult bookstore and publishing house: the Equinox Booksellers and Publishers, based in London. A serious occultist, Page oversaw the publication of a facsimile of Samuel Liddell MacGregor Mathers and Aleister Crowley's book *The Goetia*, which was faithful to the original, down to the camel-hair paper used to make the dust cover.

⟨ THAT MIC'S ON FIRE! ⟩

Guitarist Les Harvey, best known for his work with the band Stone the Crows, was killed while performing onstage in a Swansea, Wales, club on May 3, 1972. The culprit was a microphone—Harvey was grounded, and the microphone wasn't. He was electrocuted and died instantly.

⟨ IRONCLAD ⟩

The rock group Iron Maiden took its name from a medieval torture device. The most famous of these contraptions, the iron maiden of Nuremberg, was destroyed in World War II, but gruesome photographs of it remain. It consisted of a standing box with metal spikes fixed inside the doors and protruding inward from the back wall. The doors were closed slowly, effectively impaling the person inside.

> **"WHEN I LISTEN TO MUSIC, I DON'T WANT TO HEAR ABOUT FLOWERS. I LIKE DEATH AND DESTRUCTION."** —JONATHAN DAVIS

⟨ DONNA, LET'S STAY HOME ⟩

Singer-songwriter Ritchie Valens, whose hit song "Donna" topped charts in the 1950s, had a fear of airplanes long before he boarded the one that killed him in 1959. On January 31, 1957, fifteen-year-old Valens missed school to attend the funeral of his grandfather. After returning from the funeral in the afternoon, Valens's family heard a deafening explosion not far from their home. Ritchie and his brother looked to the sky just in time to see an airplane, engulfed in flames, diving to the ground. The family ran toward the wreckage to investigate and were horrified to discover that the plane had destroyed the playground of Valens's junior high school, killing three students and injuring close to a hundred others. One of the children killed was Valens's best friend, and the budding rock star was certain that he would have met the same fate had he not missed school for the funeral.

- Upwards of 75,000 die-hard fans descended on Graceland in August 2007 to observe the thirtieth anniversary of Elvis Presley's death.
- Billie Holiday, a chronic alcoholic, suffered from acute liver failure at the age of forty-four, in 1959. At the time of her hospitalization, police arrested her for possession of narcotics and kept a guard by her door until she was pronounced dead.
- John Lennon's killer, Mark David Chapman, was a church-group leader. It is said that he would lead sing-alongs to the tune of Lennon's song "Imagine," during which he would change the lyrics to "Imagine there's no John Lennon."

⟨ DEFINITELY *NOT* THE SPAWN OF THE DEVIL ⟩

Nineteenth-century violinist, guitarist, and composer Niccolo Paganini, widely considered the greatest violinist who ever lived, was said to have sold his soul to the devil for his incredible musical gift. Once, before a concert in France, the conductor asked that he bring a note from his mother confirming that his father was not, in fact, the devil. The good lady complied.

"When I started writing Sabbath stuff it was just something that sounded right. I didn't think I was going to make it Devil music." —TONY IOMMI

⟨ ROCK 'N' ROLL AND THE OCCULT ⟩

The Rolling Stones, especially Mick Jagger and Keith Richards, were deeply influenced by the occult—an interest cultivated by avant-garde filmmaker Kenneth Anger. The band came up with the concept for its hit album *Sympathy for the Devil* after reading Mikhail Bulgakov's classic *The Master and Margarita*, which is rife with satanic imagery.

Another groundbreaking rock band with rumored ties to the occult was Led Zeppelin, whose members' mythologized "pact with the devil" is well known among die-hard fans. It is said that in 1968 band members drew up a contract stating that they would follow the "left-hand path" in exchange for musical success and fame.

Some AC/DC fans claim that the band's name stands for "Anti-Christ/Devil's Children" or "After Christ the Devil Comes."

> **"YOU HAVE TO BE SAVED TO GET INTO HEAVEN . . . YOU ONLY HAVE TO BE YOU TO GET INTO HELL."** —MARILYN MANSON

⊰ BUTLER'S BOOK AND CAT ⊱

Black Sabbath's bassist, Terry Butler, was said to have psychic abilities. After Ozzy Osbourne gave him a 400-year-old book about the occult, bizarre things started happening in Butler's home. The first night he brought the book home, Butler spotted a black cat on his threshold and was convinced the cat was a ghost.

⟨ A DEATHLY ASSOCIATION ⟩

Guitarist Duane Allman of the Allman Brothers Band died in a gruesome motorcycle accident on October 29, 1971. On his way to the hospital to see Allman, the band's bassist, Barry Oakley, totaled his car. A year later, at the exact same crossroads where Allman had met his maker, Oakley was involved in another accident when his motorcycle crashed into a bus. He refused medical attention, but onlookers noticed a thin trail of blood coming out of his nose and feared he had internal damage. This proved to be the case, and Oakley died later that afternoon. Both men were twenty-four years old when they died.

⟨ DID YOU KNOW . . . ? ⟩

➤ Ronnie Van Zant, lead vocalist for Lynyrd Skynyrd, frequently played concerts barefoot, claiming that he "liked to feel the stage burn" under his feet.

➤ The scar on Johnny Cash's cheek is the result of a bungled operation to remove a cyst while he was serving in the U.S. Air Force in Germany in the 1950s.

➤ James Brown, known as the Godfather of Soul, once spent two years in prison after leading police on a high-speed car chase on Interstate 20 in Georgia.

- Otis Redding's greatest hit, "Sitting on the Dock of the Bay," was recorded just three days before the singer's plane crashed into a Wisconsin lake, killing him.
- The band Black Sabbath took its name from a 1963 horror film.
- Before he was a rock star, Rod Stewart worked as a gravedigger to pay the bills.
- Rock legend Meatloaf, born Marvin Lee Aday, got his nickname after he allowed a friend to run him over with his Volkswagen on a dare. One of his friends reportedly remarked that he "must have meatloaf for brains."
- Jimi Hendrix is said to have believed that rainbows are actually pathways that connect the living world with the dead.

⊰ ENEMIES UNTIL THE DEATH ⊱

Rockers Neil Young and Ronnie Van Zant had a complex relationship. Though the two lyricists often feuded publicly, they also held each other in high esteem. When Van Zant died, it was rumored that he was buried in a Neil Young t-shirt. Some say that his fans went so far as to exhume his body to find out, but police reports deny that his coffin was ever opened.

On October 17, 1982, members of the horror-punk band the Misfits were arrested and charged with grave robbing. The supposed target? The body of Marie Laveau, a New Orleans–based practitioner of Voodoo whose ghost is said to haunt the French Quarter to this day.

⊰ DIDN'T KNOW WHAT HIT HIM ⊱

Folk singer (and one-hit wonder, some would argue) Harry Chapin was cruising down the Long Island Expressway one day when something went wrong. According to eyewitness accounts, the singer slowed his tiny Volkwagen Beetle down to 15 mph and turned on his flashers, recklessly crossing lanes as he did so. A massive tractor-trailer, unable to slow down enough when Chapin's car cut him off, struck the Beetle, and sparks from the crash caused the car to burst into flames. The truck driver dragged Chapin's body from the wreckage shortly after, but Chapin had already died of a heart attack. Nobody knows whether the heart attack was brought on by the crash or caused it.

9. STILL ON THE BOOKS (AND IN THE ETHER)

WEIRDEST LAWS IN THE WORLD, HOAXES, AND CONSPIRACY THEORIES

⊰ DUCK DANDER ⊱

It is illegal to orally ingest duck dander in nine American states due to its intense hallucinogenic properties.

⊰ PACKED WITH PUNCH ⊱

It is currently illegal to serve sangria anywhere in Virginia. Since 1934 it has been prohibited to mix wine or beer with spirits. Because most authentic sangria is a mix of wine, liqueurs, and fruit juice, the concoction is in violation. As recently as 2006 a tapas bar in Alexandria, Virginia, was fined $2,000 for serving the illegal brew.

⊰ QUIET VIOLET ⊱

It was once against the law in France to utter the name of Napoleon's favorite flower (the violet) in public.

⊰ FISHY LAWS ⊱

Don't get a fish drunk in Oklahoma; you could go to jail. No catching whales either; that's against the law too. (Oklahoma is landlocked.)

❰ BEE LAWFUL ❱

No bees are allowed to fly in Kirkland, Illinois.

❰ WATERING HOLE ❱

The ancient Code of Hammurabi in Babylon specified that a merchant could be put to death for diluting beer.

❰ THE LAWFUL CURE ❱

Seventeenth-century lawyers are credited with the discovery of St. John's wort as a treatment for depression.

❰ ELEPHANT PROHIBITION ❱

Elephants can't drink beer in Natchez, Mississippi.

❰ YOU CAN BURN THE FLAG! ❱

In 1989 the U.S. Supreme Court conceded that burning the U.S. flag was a right protected by the First Amendment.

⟨ SMOKING ANIMALS ⟩

Don't offer a cigar, Cuban or otherwise, to any animal in Zion, Illinois. It is illegal! The law makes no mention of cigarettes or pipe tobacco.

⟨ NO CROAKING ⟩

Frogs may not croak after 11 P.M. in Memphis, Tennessee.

⟨ TREES ARE SACRED ⟩

In ancient Germany, you could be punished by death for mutilating a tree.

⟨ FULL DISCLOSURE ⟩

In July of 1991, the Supreme Court of New York State made a declaration that a home in Nyack, New York, was haunted. Why was the state's high authority brought in to rule over a matter of the supernatural? Because the couple who brought the case to court claimed that the haunting was never disclosed when they bought the house. They said the former owners or agent should have informed them of the haunting just as termite damage or any other major issue needed to be disclosed, in keeping with the law. And the haunting it-self kept the home from being inhabitable. To recoup their down payment, they took the matter to court. They were awarded damages, after the Supreme Court declared the home haunted, as a matter of law.

⟨ BUT IN IDAHO . . . ⟩

The state of Idaho has enacted a provision known as the "Ghost in the Attic" statute, which went into effect in 1998. It states that neither a home's seller nor the seller's broker is liable for not disclosing that a property may be haunted. Even if a house is the site of a known suicide or homicide, the seller need not disclose this fact *unless* the buyer specifically writes to the seller and inquires.

⟨ WYMIN IN WYOMING ⟩

In 1869, women were first granted the right to vote in the territory of Wyoming. The Nineteenth Amendment, which granted voting rights to all women in the United States, wasn't passed until 1920.

DON'T BELIEVE EVERYTHING YOU READ: "PLAINFIELD TEACHERS COLLEGE WINS AGAIN!"

➤➤ FROM THE NEW YORK HERALD TRIBUNE AND OTHER PAPERS, 1941 ◀◀

The story: In 1941 the *Herald Tribune*, the *New York Post*, and a number of other New York papers began reporting the scores of a New Jersey football team called the Plainfield Teachers College Flying Figments as it battled teams like Harmony Teachers College and Appalachia Tech for a coveted invitation to the first-ever Blackboard Bowl.

The reaction: As the season progressed and the Figments remained undefeated, interest in the small college powerhouse grew—and so did the press coverage. Several papers ran feature articles on Johnny Chung, the team's "stellar Chinese halfback who has accounted for 69 of Plainfield's 117 points."

The truth: Plainfield, the Flying Figments, and its opponents were all invented by a handful of bored New York stockbrokers who were amazed that real teams from places like Slippery Rock got their scores into big-city newspapers. Each Saturday, the brokers phoned in fake scores, then waited for them to appear in the Sunday papers. The hoax lasted nearly the entire season, until *Time* magazine got wind of it and decided to run a story.

⟨ THE ACCIDENTAL TOURIST ⟩

A tourist visiting San Francisco in 1964 was involved in a minor cable car accident. As a result, she sued the city of San Francisco, claiming that the incident had turned her into a nymphomaniac. She won the case and received an award of $50,000.

⟨ NO POPPIES PLEASE ⟩

Opium was legal in the United States until 1942.

RELAXATION TECHNIQUES ⟨ CAN BE BAD FOR YOU ⟩

Don't fall asleep in the bathtub in Detroit. You could be arrested, because sleeping in bathtubs is illegal in the city.

⟨ THREE CHEERS ⟩

You need at least three people to make a legal riot.

⟨ LATE NIGHT PEANUTS ⟩

Buying peanuts after sundown in Alabama is illegal.

⟨ CEMETERY SPACE-SAVER ⟩

It is against the law to bury an intact body in Japan. Ashes with body parts or bits of bone in them are fine.

⟨ THE DEVIL IN THE COURTROOM ⟩

Pennsylvanian law books record a 1971 case of a man suing Satan—for his own bad luck and downfall. The case was thrown out of court on the grounds that Satan did not live in the state of Pennsylvania.

⟨ HIGH SEAS INLAND ⟩

The U.S. Supreme Court classifies the Great Lakes for shipping as it does other large bodies of water: as high seas.

⟨ CIVIL TAXATION ⟩

United States income tax was originally enacted to raise money during the Civil War. Although the U.S. Supreme Court voted to remove the income tax after the war, Congress reinstated it in 1913.

⟨ IS THAT A BOTTLE IN YOUR POCKET . . . ? ⟩

In South Carolina hip pockets are illegal, as they provide convenient places to hide a pint bottle or flask.

⟨ KENTUCKY COMMANDMENTS ⟩

In Kentucky, several unusual laws still prevail:

- A state law mandates people bathe at least once a year.
- Anyone who throws eggs or tomatoes at a public speaker will be sentenced to a year in prison.
- Females in bathing suits are not allowed on any highway, unless they are escorted by two officers armed with a club. This law does not apply to females weighing less than ninety pounds or those exceeding two hundred pounds; nor does it apply to female horses.

> It is against the law to dye chicks, ducklings, or baby rabbits, unless offering six or more of them for sale and at the same time.

⟨ WHISTLE WHILE YOU WADE ⟩

In Vermont it is illegal to whistle underwater.

⟨ LYING IN LAKE ⟩

In Lake Charles, Louisiana, it is illegal to let a rain puddle remain in your front yard for more than twelve hours.

THE CIA AND LSD

▶⟩ NAZI HALLUCINOGENICS ⟨◀

During World War II, Nazi scientists tested hallucinogenic drugs (such as mescaline) on inmates at the Dachau concentration camp. The Nazis were ostensibly trying to find a new "aviation medicine," but what they were really looking for was the secret to mind control.

After dosing inmates for years, the Nazi scientists concluded that mind control was impossible, even when strong doses of the hallucinogens had been given to their patients. But they did find that they could extract the most intimate of secrets from subjects under a drug's influence.

━━━ ▶ THE CIA TAKES OVER THE TRIP, MAN ◀ ━━━

After the war, U.S. military intelligence found out about the Nazi experiments and wondered if hallucinogenic drugs might be used for espionage. Could such drugs be sprayed over enemy armies to disable them? Could they be used to confuse or discredit leaders in hostile countries? The possibilities seemed endless, and in 1950, the Central Intelligence Agency (CIA) took over where the Nazis had left off.

In 1953, the CIA initiated a full-scale mind-control program called Operation MK-ULTRA. Its experiments studied the potential effects of hypnosis, electroshocks, extrasensory perception (ESP), lobotomy, and drugs. The operation is said to have lasted twenty years and cost $25 million.

According to the book *Acid Dreams: The CIA, LSD, and the Sixties Rebellion* by Martin A. Lee and Bruce Shalin, "Nearly every drug that appeared on the black market during the 1960's—marijuana, cocaine, PCP, DMT, speed, and many others—had previously been scrutinized, tested, and in some cases refined by the CIA and army scientists. But . . . none received as much attention or was embraced with such enthusiasm as LSD-25 [lysergic acid diethylamide]. For a time, CIA personnel were completely infatuated with the hallucinogen. Those who first tested LSD in the early 1950s were convinced that it would revolutionize the cloak-and-dagger trade."

In order to find out if the drug was effective as a secret weapon, the CIA first had to test it—on people.

━━━ ►➤ THE SECRET LSD TESTS ◄◄ ━━━

In 1973, the CIA destroyed most of its files on the MK-ULTRA project, but some files escaped destruction. From these files, Congress and the public learned, for the first time, that for years the CIA had been experimenting with drugs.

To test LSD, the CIA had set up both secret operations and academic fronts. For instance, it established a "Society for the Investigation of Human Ecology," at the Cornell University medical school, which dispensed "grants" to institutions in the U.S. and Canada to conduct experiments with LSD.

The LSD project was actually administered by the CIA's technical services staff. A freewheeling atmosphere developed in which anyone was likely to be dosed without warning in the name of research. Before the program concluded, thousands of people had been involuntarily dosed.

In a San Francisco operation code-named Midnight Climax, prostitutes brought men to bordellos that were actually CIA safe houses. They would spike the men's drinks once inside the bordellos, and when they were properly affected, CIA operatives would observe, photograph, and record the action that ensued.

In another experiment, black inmates at the Lexington Narcotics Hospital were given LSD for seventy-five consecutive days in gradually decreasing doses.

The U.S. Army was also involved in LSD experiments. *Acid Dreams* reports that in the 1950s "nearly fifteen hundred military personnel had served as human guinea pigs in LSD experiments conducted by the US Army Chemical Corps." The army even made a film of troops trying to drill while tripping on acid.

Eventually, the government had no choice but to admit it had given LSD to about one thousand unsuspecting people from 1955 to 1958 and has paid millions of dollars to settle lawsuits that were filed when subjects given drugs became permanently incapacitated or committed suicide.

For example, one lawsuit involved a civilian who, while working for the army in 1953, was slipped LSD at a CIA party. He then jumped to his death from a tenth-story window. His was originally ruled a suicide, but in 1975 the government finally revealed that he had been intentionally drugged the night he died. The CIA apologized, and Congress awarded his family $750,000.

Another case described how a CIA-funded psychiatrist in Canada dosed patients with LSD and used other mind-control techniques, in an attempt to "reprogram" them. Nine of the patients later sued the CIA for damages. The case was settled out of court in 1988.

THE OSWALD CONNECTION

Was Lee Harvey Oswald one of those given LSD by the CIA? As a seventeen-year-old marine, Oswald was assigned to the U.S. naval air base in Atsugi, Japan, in 1957. It has been said that this base was one of two overseas stations where the CIA conducted LSD testing.

10. PASSING STRANGE

ABERRATIONS, FASCINATING PHOBIAS,
AND ODD ANCIENT BELIEFS

⟨ FACES ONLY A MOTHER COULD LOVE ⟩

Krao was a "wild child" who lived in Europe in the 1880s. Sometimes known as "Darwin's missing link," she sported a prognathic face (one where the lower jaw extends beyond the upper part of the face), and her head and face were covered with a thick mane of hair down to the neck. Krao was first put on exhibit in a freak show when she was just seven years old. She was known for throwing temper tantrums, during which she would writhe on the ground and attempt to pull the hair out of her face.

Jo-Jo the Dog-Faced Boy was an early 1900s freak-show performer who was said to have been captured in the forests of Russia, where he had been living off berries and small animals in imitation of his neighbors, the wolves. In reality he was just a very hairy boy, like his father, who was exhibited as a dog-faced man. Both father and son had thick, sandy-colored hair growing in tufts all over their faces. They were said to resemble terriers and had mastered a very convincing barking routine.

The hirsute Krao and Jo-Jo may have suffered from a rare genetic disorder called congenital hypertrichosis. People afflicted with this condition, of which there are only about fifty documented cases since the Middle Ages, are covered head to toe with hair.

⟨ MAXIMUM MASS ⟩

Roman Emperor Maximus was the legendary king who was so large that he could wear his wife's bracelet as a wedding ring. He was said to be between eight and nine feet tall, and was a compulsive eater, binging on four pounds of flesh and six gallons of wine a day. He was as much muscle as he was fat, though, as he was known to be capable of knocking out the teeth of a horse with a single blow.

"I have three phobias which, could I mute them, would make my life as slick as a sonnet, but as dull as ditch water: I hate to go to bed, I hate to get up, and I hate to be alone." —TALLULAH BANKHEAD

⟨ CHOREOMANIA ⟩

At various times in different countries, actual epidemics of dancing mania have occurred. In the fourteenth and fifteenth centuries, these epidemics were especially common in western Germany. They would begin in an isolated community and in a short time would spread over a wide area. Soon whole communities across wide areas would be engaging in frenzied dancing.

⟨ MOM, I FEEL SICK ⟩

Scholionophobia is an extreme fear and hatred of school.

⟨ DON'T JUMP! ⟩

If you have a fear of falling from a height to your death, you have a mild version of bathophobia. This is not an uncommon fear, but the manic phobia manifests in a fear of not being able to control an impulse to jump from a high place.

⟨ DOCTOR, I'M NOT WELL ⟩

If you were really craving a drink during Prohibition, there was a clause in the Eighteenth Amendment that allowed for the use of alcohol for medicinal purposes.

Medicines that contained alcohol were prescribed for any number of "illnesses."

⟨ SCARY HAIR ⟩

Katharine Hepburn suffered from a phobia of dirty hair. When she was shooting films for Twentieth Century Fox, she would sniff the heads of the cast and crew to make sure their hair was squeaky clean.

⟨ XENOGLOSSIA ⟩

Xenoglossia is the act of spontaneously speaking in a strange or foreign language without having learned it or having been exposed to it, but with the added implication of extreme revulsion or distaste to this linguistic act. The ability to speak in a foreign tongue may be an evidence for reincarnation and may occur when a person is reliving a past life. The linguistic act sometimes can be as simple as a few words or phrases, or in some instances, an entire fluent conversation being carried out in a language the person is not even aware exists. In some of the most credible and compelling cases of xenoglossia recorded, the subject not only spoke in a foreign language, but also used an archaic version of it that had not been in regular usage for centuries, making it extremely unlikely that the ability was a fantasy or a hoax.

⟨ DELUSIONS, MANIAS, AND PHOBIAS ⟩

➤ Erotographomania is the overwhelming drive to write love letters.

➤ Echolalia is the senseless repetition of words or sounds.

➤ Liticaphobia is the fear of lawsuits.

➤ Thanatomania is a neurotic obsession with attending funerals and reading obituaries.

➤ Cachinnation is senseless laughter, as found in manic-depression and certain types of schizophrenia.

➤ Thanatophobia is a morbid fear of death. If you experience a morbid fear of darkness, you are nyctophobic.

➤ Nosophobia is fear of illness.

➤ Mysophobia is the irrational fear of dirt and germs. Mysophobics usually spend an inordinate amount of time washing their hands, and many have trouble leaving the house.

➤ If you have an unreasonable fear of experiencing pain, you are algophobic.

➤ Theomania is a morbid fear of religious cults.

- If you believe you have been transformed into a wolf, you are suffering from the delusion of lycanthropy.
- Ophidiophobia is the fear of snakes and snakelike creatures.
- Ereuthophobia is the morbid fear of blushing.
- Alcoholomania is an irresistible craving for alcoholic drinks, while letheomania is a morbid craving for drugs.
- Eisoptrophobia is the excessive fear of mirrors.
- Taphephobia is a morbid fear of being buried alive.
- Anaphia is the loss of the sense of pressure.
- Cacophobia is the fear of ugliness. People with this phobia tend to avoid ugly people and asymmetrical objects.
- The impulse to disrobe in public is known as asecdysiasm.
- Aritmophobia is the fear of numbers. Sufferers of this condition often have trouble with their finances, reading simple traffic signs, and understanding pricing systems at stores.

⤙ PERSONAL PARALYSIS ⤚

Abasia is a loss of the power to walk when there are no structural or organic changes to account for the inability to move. Abasiac individuals are utterly convinced that they are not capable of movement and that if they attempt to walk something terrible is going to happen to them or to someone around them.

⟨ BLESS ME, FATHER ⟩

A person suffering from agonia experiences extreme grief due to delusions of having committed the original sin.

⟨ FALL FROM GRACE ⟩

Basophobia is the fear of standing up or attempting to walk, stemming mainly from of a fear that one will then fall.

⟨ QUIVERING THUNDER ⟩

The extreme dread of thunder is called brontophobia. For brontophobes, the boom and crash of thunder has a demonic quality. Often found in people suffering from a psychoneurosis, brontophobia can also be associated with a person, often a person in a position of authority, and the fearsome thunder is their expression of disapproval.

⟨ CONSPIRACY OF BEARDS ⟩

Pogonophobia is the fear of beards.

⟨ TOO MUCH ECHO ⟩

Cenophobia is primarily a morbid fear of empty rooms, but also encompasses a fear of large halls, auditoriums, and edifices with high ceilings.

⟨ MELON HEADS ⟩

Many lifelong residents of Kirkland, Ohio, grew up listening to tales of melon heads, a strange race of local mutants. Local legend has it that these people, known for their oversized, bulbous craniums, are the result of a physician's bizarre experiments on children suffering from a debilitating disease called hydrocephalus. This condition causes large pockets of water to form in the brain, and Dr. Crow was hired by the U.S. government to investigate and care for children with the disorder. Instead, he performed twisted operations on his patients, injecting their brains with more water and exposing them to radiation. Many children died, and the remaining victims mutated into wild, vicious creatures. One day they attacked the doctor, ripped him to pieces, and ate him. Then they unleashed themselves on the woods around the crude hospital they had been imprisoned in. The story goes that the melon heads roam the woods in packs, terrorizing humans and animals alike.

⟨ THE NUMBER THIRTEEN ⟩

Triskaidekaphobia is a morbid fear of the number thirteen or the date Friday the thirteenth.

In early Christianity, the number thirteen was considered unlucky because it was the number of persons present at the Last Supper, and Friday unlucky because Christ was said to have been crucified on a Friday.

11. THE VAPORS

MEDICAL MALADIES AND CURIOUS CURES

⟨ BRAIN-EATING AMOEBAS ⟩

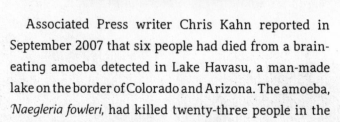

Associated Press writer Chris Kahn reported in September 2007 that six people had died from a brain-eating amoeba detected in Lake Havasu, a man-made lake on the border of Colorado and Arizona. The amoeba, *Naegleria fowleri*, had killed twenty-three people in the United States between 1995 and 2004.

The amoeba thrives in warm waters, and infectious levels have been detected in lakes, hot springs, and even dirty swimming pools. When infected water gets into the body through the nose, the amoeba is able to travel up the olfactory nerve to the brain, destroying tissue along the way. Once within the brain, it begins to feed on brain cells.

⟨ ALTERNATIVE MEDICINE ⟩

State-of-the-art medicine in prehistoric times was designed to keep alien demon spirits from infecting the body. Preventive medicine included magic, charms,

incantations, and talismans. If, despite preventive measures, demons entered a patient's body, prehistoric medical personnel drove out the malicious spirits by inducing violent vomiting. If that didn't work, making the body inhospitable to the spirit was the next step; caregivers would begin a regimen of beating, torturing, and starving the patient. For especially resistant demons, a hole drilled into the patient's head was prescribed to encourage the demon to escape.

⊰ SAINTLY WOMAN ⊱

Apollonia is the patron saint of toothache sufferers. That's because in A.D. 249, the Romans tortured her by pulling out all her teeth in an attempt to get her to forsake Christianity. She didn't and saved the Romans the task of burning her at the stake by jumping into the fire of her own accord. Her teeth and jaws are now on display at churches throughout Europe.

⊰ NEVERENDING HICCUPS ⊱

In January 2007, Jennifer Mee, a fifteen-year-old from Florida, got the hiccups. For more than three weeks, she continued to hiccup, close to fifty times a minute, despite trying many home remedies and consulting doctors. She held her breath; she put sugar under her tongue. She breathed into a paper bag and tried drinking out of the wrong side of a glass. She had blood tests and an MRI. Nothing worked—not even various people's attempts to scare the hiccups out of her. Why the hiccups began and what they were a symptom of could not be determined.

⟨ HIDDEN LIMBS ⟩

In 2007, in Maiden, North Carolina, a man bought a smoker at a police auction of abandoned items from a storage facility. When he opened up the smoker, he discovered what he thought was wood wrapped up in paper. The bundle instead turned out to be a human leg that had been amputated at just above the knee. Police contacted the owners of the storage facility. It turned out that the owner's son had had his leg amputated after a plane crash and kept the leg for "religious reasons." She and her son drove some thirty-five miles to retrieve it from the man who had bought the smoker.

⟨ GEORGE WASHINGTON'S TEETH ⟩

Contrary to popular myth, George Washington didn't have wooden teeth. He had four sets of dentures made from a mix of hippopotamus bone, elephant ivory, and the teeth from cows and dead people. None of them worked well, and the discomfort of his dentures is one reason he looks so sour in his portraits.

"Madness is tonic and invigorating. It makes the sane more sane. The only ones who are unable to profit by it are the insane." —HENRY MILLER

⟨ MAGGOT ACT ⟩

Investigators in Tacoma, Washington, were able to identify two generations of maggots on a body that had died by a gunshot wound. In doing so, they determined the approximate date of the corpse's demise, as a maggot's life cycle lasts only about three weeks. Armed with the estimated date of death, the investigators were able to trace the deceased's whereabouts and eventually find the killer.

⊰ FULL STOMACH ⊱

The Northern State Hospital for the Insane, in Oshkosh, Wisconsin, boasts one of the more bizarre exhibits in museum history—a collection of artifacts that patients have swallowed during the asylum's 150-year history. Among the items are scissors, a bedspring, a toothbrush, and a thermometer. Also featured are twenty-six spoons that were all swallowed by one man.

⊰ MYSTERY CURE ⊱

It's easy to laugh at outlandish folk medicines of the past, but consider this: In 2001, a mysterious ancient Chinese potion made of ground rock and toad venom was investigated as a promising experimental cancer treatment at Sloane-Kettering Hospital in New York City. Scientists had no idea why, but the arsenic trioxide in the potion appeared to cure a particularly devastating kind of leukemia.

⊰ PRESERVATIVES ⊱

Today's morticians report that dead bodies don't decom-pose as fast as they used to. They speculate the change is due to people eating food containing so many more preservatives than food of the past.

> **MORE THAN 700 MILLION PEOPLE WORLDWIDE HOST A BLOOD-SUCKING HOOKWORM IN THEIR BODIES.**

⟨ THREE-LEGGED WONDER ⟩

Francesco Lentini was born in 1889 with what appeared to be a tail but which was in fact a nearly developed foot growing from the base of his spine. Although he was treated as a disabled outcast most of his life, he found work in Italian sideshows and was quoted as having said, "I have never complained. I think life is beautiful, and I enjoy living it." He lived to the ripe age of seventy-eight.

⟨ HEALING JEWELS ⟩

Originally, earrings were worn to guard the ears from illness. Earrings, particularly diamond earrings, were also believed to help eyesight. Wearing one silver and one gold earring was believed to be a cure for headaches.

⟨ STRANGE VIRGIN BIRTH ⟩

During World War II a young woman in Germany, Emmie Marie Jones, gave birth to a daughter, despite the fact that she insisted she was a virgin. In 1955, scientists in England did genetic testing and discovered that Emmie and her daughter were genetically identical twins. The only explanation the scientists could offer was that the shock of the bombing caused partheno-genesis, the spontaneous splitting of an unfertilized egg.

> IN 1938, NEW YORK BECAME THE FIRST STATE TO PASS A LAW THAT REQUIRED MEDICAL TESTS FOR MARRIAGE-LICENSE APPLICANTS.

⟨ GET PREGNANT, STOP ARTHRITIS ⟩

No one knows why, but pregnancy is known to alleviate the stiffness of arthritis.

⟨ MOVE OVER, GENE SIMMONS ⟩

A disease called hypertrophy causes the tongue to enlarge. Once enlarged, it may become too big for the mouth and can grow long enough to reach one's chest. Side effects include possible deformity of the teeth and mouth, and the afflicted person may choke on her or his tongue.

EVERY PERSON HAS A UNIQUE TONGUE PRINT.

⟨ ESCAPE THE COLD ⟩

If you're ever desperate for a winter free of the common cold and flu, go to the North Pole. It's impossible to catch a cold there, because the air is too frigid for the microorganisms that foster colds to survive.

⟨ DID YOU KNOW . . . ? ⟩

> One in five women suffer from migraines.
> The human body contains 32 million bacteria per square inch.
> Our bodies are ever evolving. Our little toes and appendixes are getting smaller because we don't need them, and our teeth are shrinking in size due to the amount of processed and cooked foods we consume.

- The average human will shed about 1.5 pounds of skin particles every year, and by seventy years of age, that adds up to 105 pounds.
- Humans lose and then regenerate their outer epidermis about every month, making almost a thousand new skins in an average life span.
- The human body is composed of around 10 trillion cells. On any given day three billion of those cells die and are replaced, except for the ones in your brain. Once they die, they are gone forever.
- The rarest blood type is type A-H and has been found in less than a dozen people.
- A person will die from total lack of sleep sooner than from starvation. Death will occur after about ten days without sleep, while starvation takes a few weeks.
- A sneeze can exceed 100 mph.
- Beards are the fastest growing hairs on the human body.
- Fingernails grow faster than toenails.
- The brain is composed of 85 percent water, and its consistency is somewhere between that of jelly and cooked pasta.
- Three hundred million cells die in the human body every minute.

- If stretched out, the human small intestine would measure twenty-two feet long.
- Arriazia is a disorder that prevents women from growing breasts.

⟨ WHEN I GROW UP, I WANT TO BE A PINEAPPLE ⟩

Contagious follicular keratosis causes the sufferers to grow small, yellow, spiny growths all over the body.

⟨ EVERY MAN'S DREAM COME TRUE ⟩

Men with diphallic terata have not one but two penises.

⟨ GIVING BINGING A NEW MEANING ⟩

A starving fashion model who had been purging in order to look svelte for a photo shoot began to eat frantically after the shoot was completed. She ate a whopping nineteen pounds of food in all—and the stomach can only hold four quarts of liquid. Her stomach ruptured, killing her instantly.

THE BOOK OF THE BIZARRE

⟨ LIFELONG BAD HAIR DAYS ⟩

Hair becomes irreversibly tangled and eventually becomes matted, at which point it may also become sticky, foul-smelling, and cause scalp inflammation. This condition, called Plica, or Polish ringworm, was discovered in Poland and is known to affect primarily Polish people.

THE GIANT LEAP FORWARD ⟨ THAT'S KEEPING YOU DOWN ⟩

Any time people with a Saltatoric spasm try to stand, they are forced to jump about uncontrollably due to muscular spasms that contract their calves, hips, knees, and back.

⟨ MODERN-DAY ZOMBIE ⟩

Narcolepsy, an uncommon sleep disorder, is a state of perpetual exhaustion. Contrary to common belief, a narcoleptic is not going to fall asleep randomly or in midsentence while speaking. However, if someone else dominates the conversation and bores them for long enough, narcoleptics may very well fall asleep. Side effects of narcolepsy include cataplexy (complete loss of muscle tone), hallucinations, and caffeine resistance.

⟨ SKULL TRAPS ⟩

Trepanation is defined as the practice of removing a portion of the skull to expose the brain. It's been practiced for thousands of years, both for medical reasons and as a means of achieving enlightenment. Archaeologists in France have found a 7,000-year-old skull that had undergone trepanation, and the procedure was practiced by the ancient Egyptians, Chinese, Indians, Romans, and Greeks.

⟨ JOB'S SYNDROME ⟩

Lesions that form on the skin, in the sinuses, and in the lungs are part of a condition called Job's syndrome, which is named for the biblical character who was covered with boils. It predominantly affects red-haired females, but everyone is susceptible to the odd disease.

⟨ ELEPHANT MAN ⟩

Joseph Merrick, also known as the Elephant Man, was a sideshow performer in Europe during the 1880s. He was rescued by Dr. Frederick Treves, who called his condition Elephant man disease and wrote the definitive book, *The Elephant Man and Other Reminiscences*, about him. Treves described Merrick as "deformed in body, face, head, and limbs," noting that "his skin, thick and pendulous, hung in folds and resembled the hide of an elephant."

Merrick was mistreated for most of his life, and when sideshows were outlawed in 1886, he was out of work and virtually unemployable because of his looks. After Merrick suffered from an acute bronchial infection in a train station, Treves was contacted, and he put Merrick under his care and study. The elephant man was well received in Victorian society; a kind of novelty, he was well mannered and interesting, and became a favorite of Queen Victoria. He died at the age of twenty-seven after dislocating his neck in his sleep.

> **"I FIND THE MEDICINE WORSE THAN THE MALADY."** —JOHN FLETCHER

12. SUPERSTITIONS AND CURSES

TO HEX, LAMBAST, AND BEWITCH

"Double, double, toil and trouble;

Fire burn and cauldron bubble.

Fillet of a fenny snake,

In the cauldron boil and bake;

Eye of newt and toe of frog,

Wool of bat and tongue of dog,

Adder's fork and blind-worm's sting,

Lizard's leg and howlet's wing,

For a charm of pow'rful trouble,

Like a hell-broth boil and bubble."

—WILLIAM SHAKESPEARE, *MACBETH*

≺ FINDING A FOUR-LEAF CLOVER ≻

The belief that four-leaf clovers are good luck comes from the Druids, ancient residents of the British Isles. Several times a year, they gathered in oak groves to settle legal disputes and offer sacrifices. They ended their gatherings by hunting for four-leaf clovers because they believed a four-leaf enabled its owner to see evil spirits and witches—and therefore avoid these things.

⟨ THROWING PENNIES INTO A WELL ⟩

Some ancient people believed spirits living in springs and fountains demanded tributes—usually tributes of flesh. Young Mayan girls, for example, were sometimes tossed into the Well of Sacrifice (where they would "marry" the spirits). Today, people just toss the spirits a penny or two for luck.

⟨ KNOCKING ON WOOD ⟩

In the Middle Ages, churchmen insisted that knocking on wood was part of their tradition of prayer, since Christ was crucified on a wooden cross. But the tradition of knocking on wood actually started several thousands of years earlier, with a different deity. Both Native Americans and ancient Greeks developed the belief (independently) that oak trees were the domain of an important god. By knocking on an oak, they were communicating with the god and asking for his forgiveness. The Greeks passed their tradition on to the Romans, and it became part of European lore. The oak's power was eventually transferred to all types of wood.

⟨ OPENING AN UMBRELLA INDOORS ⟩

In the eighteenth century, spring-loaded, metal-spoked umbrellas were new and unpredictable. Opening one indoors was courting disaster—the open umbrella could fly out of control and damage property or people. Therefore, opening an umbrella indoors was considered not so much bad luck as just dangerous.

⟨ MIRRORS ⟩

Long ago, people looked at their reflections in water and were amazed because they thought they were glimpsing their soul. When the reflected image was altered by waves or ripples, they thought that their soul was in danger. Over time, this belief morphed into the belief that if someone broke a mirror, it would take seven years for their soul to return to them. The term of seven years was established by the Romans, who believed it took a body seven years to repair itself. These beliefs eventually became the superstition that breaking a mirror means seven years of bad luck.

Another superstition says that should a mirror fall and break on its own, a death in the home is soon to be expected. Even the house where the mirror breaks is thought to be cursed for seven years. Looking at your reflection in a mirror by candlelight is also said to bring bad luck.

> **"SUPERSTITION BRINGS THE GODS INTO EVEN THE SMALLEST MATTERS." —TITUS LIVY**

⟨ CANDLES ⟩

- Candles are shrouded in mystery and superstition. First of all, beware of a candle that blows out during a ceremony. It's a warning that evil is nearby.
- Three lit candles in a row are bad luck, so be sure to blow one out if you see them.
- Light a candle inside a jack-o'-lantern on Halloween to guard against evil spirits that are lurking about.
- If you look into a mirror by candlelight, you not only risk giving yourself bad luck, but you also may find the souls of the dead.
- A corpse candle is a small, sourceless flame that floats through the night air and is believed to be a lost soul. This sight is considered an omen of death.

⟨ SALT ⟩

For thousands of years, superstitions about salt have been incorporated into religious, domestic, and business practices. Because salt could preserve food, people thought it had the power to protect them as well. Salt was poured into wells to purify water against evil and placed on the chest of a corpse before burial. Mothers even salted their babies, believing salt would lengthen their lives.

In biblical times, people ate salt to ensure that business agreements would remain true. But salt was not always considered good luck—it was forbidden to speak the word "salt" while at sea for fear of the consequences.

In supernatural workings, salt is also relied upon. It is often placed in the corners of a room before a spell is cast, and people often take ritual salt baths to break harmful spells put upon them. It is also understood that when we spill salt, friendly spirits to our right are warning us that evil approaches on the left; tossing a pinch of salt over the left shoulder staves off danger.

⟨ GUESTS ⟩

Hundreds of years ago, people traveled very little. Communities were fearful of the world that existed beyond the boundaries of their villages. Witches and ominous gods were thought to live among the surrounding mountains, valleys, and seas. People believed that the stranger knocking on their door could be a spirit in disguise. If not treated hospitably, the spirit could cast an evil spell on a home. So families welcomed strangers and treated them well, providing them with food and comfort, so that the spirit-stranger would leave their homes in peace when he or she moved on.

⟨ LADDERS ⟩

Historical explanations seem to justify the superstition that walking under a ladder brings bad luck. To the ancient Egyptians, the triangular shape of pyramids was sacred, and to walk under a ladder would be to break the triangle it formed with the wall. This act, they believed, would have deadly consequences.

The Christians believed that the triangle formed by a ladder leaning against a wall represented the Holy Trinity (the Father, Son [Jesus Christ], and Holy Ghost). If you were to walk under the ladder, you would be violating the Holy Trinity. It was also feared that when you walked through the ladder-based triangle, you walked with the devil.

In more recent times, tall ladders were used to take down the corpse from the noose after someone had been hanged. It was believed that if you walked under that ladder, the dead person, swinging from the gallows above, would watch you pass, and then you, too, would meet your death. It was also feared that the body would fall onto those who crossed below the ladder.

⊰ HUNGARIAN VIEWS ⊱

Traditional Hungarian culture is rich with superstitions. Here are a few of the most prominent, recorded by famed Hungarian witch Zsuzsanna Budapest in her book *The Holy Book of Women's Mysteries*:

- If your left palm itches, money is coming to you; if the right itches, you will soon spend the money.
- If salt is spilled from its container, let the one who upset the container clean it up. Otherwise poverty will strike the house, bringing great fights over money issues.
- If you place a loaf of bread upside down on a table, there will be fights in the home.
- If your nose itches, you have adversities.
- If you are traveling to visit someone without an appointment and a bird flies across your path, forget the visit; the person will not be home.

⊰ BROOMS ⊱

There are many superstitions surrounding brooms. You should avoid placing a broom against your bed because the broom's evil spirit will cast a spell on the bed. Don't let a broom sweep over your feet if you ever wish to be married, and never step over the handle of a broom lying on the floor because doing so is believed to bring death. If you drop a broom, company will arrive. If you sweep trash out your door at night, it summons the visit of a stranger. And if you forget to sweep out the room where an unwelcome guest has stayed, that guest may return. To prevent additional bad luck, never take an old broom with you when you move.

⊰ THE BLACK CAT ⊱

The black cat is the most common enchanted animal of the mystical world. Often the companions of witches, black cats are believed to have the power to reason, perform sorcery, and understand human languages.

Just about everyone knows the superstition that says when a black cat crosses your path, bad luck will follow. But there are ways to counteract this omen. As soon as you spot the black cat, spit on the ground, turn yourself around three times, or walk backwards retracing your steps. As you pass the cat, reach down and stroke its back as a gesture of kindness.

⟨ VAMPIRES ⟩

Vampires first appeared in Slavic folktales about one thousand years ago. Villagers blamed disease and death—which were completely mysterious in those days—on corpses that only came out at night and sucked people's blood. Eager to rid the village of this malevolence, people often dug up graves and dispatched those corpses that bore signs of being a vampire; by impaling the body's heart with a stake or beheading the body, the vampire could be permanently put to rest. To keep the undead out of the house, garlic and religious symbols were thought to work. The undead could also be destroyed by exposure to daylight.

Over the years, the vampires of legend have acquired various characteristics, such as superhuman strength and speed, hypnotic mind-control abilities, and inhuman stealth. But you'll notice that many details of the old superstition remain to this day.

"EVIL IS JUST A POINT OF VIEW." —ANNE RICE

⟨ AFTERBIRTH: BURNING PLACENTAS ⟩

In the seventeenth century, midwives had a custom of saving a woman's afterbirth, or placenta, and then burning it. The superstition was that the number of times the burning placenta popped indicated the number of children the mother could expect to have in the future.

⟨ APPLE BLOSSOMS ⟩

An apple blossom is said to be a sure sign of sickness in a house. If you are superstitious, never bring a branch of an apple blossom into your home.

⟨ ASH TREES AND CALAMITIES ⟩

In the nineteenth century, every summer some people would examine ash trees to see whether or not they produced any seed. The barrenness of an ash tree was said to be a sure sign of public calamity. Aged and wise men maintained that the ash trees of England produced no seeds in 1649, the year in which King Charles I was beheaded.

> **IF THIRTEEN PEOPLE SIT DOWN TO EAT AT A TABLE TOGETHER, ONE OF THEM WILL DIE WITHIN THE YEAR.**

⊰ BABY MAGIC ⊱

It has been said that if a baby looks at you from between its legs, you will get pregnant.

⊰ BATS: FRIEND OR FOE? ⊱

In the nineteenth century, it was said that if a live bat were carried three times around the house and then nailed outside of the window with its head downwards, it would have the effects of a countercharm. Nowadays, it is considered lucky if you see a bat flying around on its own in the daytime, but if you disturb a bat and make it fly, you will have bad luck. Even more disturbing is the belief that a bat coming into the house is a sure sign of an impending death in the family.

⟨ BEANS, BEANS, BAD FOR THE MIND ⟩

> Sleep in a bean field all night if you want to have awful dreams, or even worse, go crazy.

> A common superstition among miners says that accidents in the mining pit occur more frequently when bean fields are in bloom.

⟨ BED LORE ⟩

> It is said one should never sleep with his or her feet toward the door, because only corpses lie like that.

> Some believe that it is unlucky to get out of bed backwards.

> In Scotland, there is the belief that it is unlucky to leave a bed while making it. If the bed-making is interrupted, the occupant of the bed will pass a sleepless night, or some much worse evil will befall him or her.

> Some believe that if three people take part in making a bed, there is sure to be a death in the house within the year.

> IF SOMEBODY IS ILL AND SUDDENLY ASKS FOR A MUG OF
> HARD CIDER, HE OR SHE WILL SOON DIE.

⟨ SUPERSTITIONS OF THE RICH AND FAMOUS ⟩

▶ JOHN MADDEN ◀

When John Madden was coach of the Oakland Raiders football team, he wouldn't let the team leave the locker room until running back Mark van Eeghen had belched.

▶ STONEWALL JACKSON ◀

Confederate general Thomas "Stonewall" Jackson always charged into battle with his left hand held over his head, allegedly for psychic balance.

▶ ALFRED HITCHCOCK ◀

The cameo appearance Alfred Hitchcock made in each film he directed was for good luck.

▶ MICHAEL JORDAN ◀

Former Chicago Bulls star Michael Jordan always wore the shorts from his college basketball uniform under his professional uniform. "As long as I have these shorts on . . . I feel confident," he said.

> **IT IS BELIEVED THAT IF YOU CRY ON YOUR BIRTHDAY, YOU WILL CONTINUE TO CRY YEAR ROUND.**

►❯ THE BARRYMORES ❮◄

Lionel, Ethel, and John Barrymore always gave each other an apple on the night of a show's premiere.

►❯ JIMMY CONNORS ❮◄

Jimmy Connors wouldn't compete in a tennis match without a little note from his grandma tucked into his sock.

►❯ JACK LEMMON ❮◄

The late actor Jack Lemmon always whispered "magic time" as filming started on a new movie.

►❯ THOMAS EDISON ❮◄

American inventor Thomas Edison carried a staurolite, a stone that forms naturally in the shape of a cross. Legend has it that when fairies heard of Christ's crucifixion, their tears fell as these "fairy cross" stones.

Staurolite was also a lucky stone for U.S. presidents Theodore Roosevelt and Woodrow Wilson.

►❯ GRETA GARBO ❮◄

Actress Greta Garbo always wore a lucky string of pearls.

►❯ MARIO ANDRETTI ❮◄

Race-car driver Mario Andretti won't use a green pen to sign autographs.

►❯ KICHIRO TOYODA ❮◄

A fortune-teller told businessman Kichiro Toyoda that it would be good luck to change his company's name to *Toyota* and give the company's cars names beginning with the letter *C* (such as Celica and Camry).

►❯ JOHN WAYNE ❮◄

Actor John Wayne considered it lucky to be in a movie with fellow actor Ward Bond.

> **"SUPERSTITION IS THE POETRY OF LIFE, SO THAT IT DOES NOT INJURE THE POET TO BE SUPERSTITIOUS."** —JOHANN WOLFGANG VON GOETHE

JOHN MCENROE

Tennis player John McEnroe thinks it is bad luck to play a match on a Thursday the twelfth. He also carefully avoids stepping on a white line of the tennis court.

RANDY JOHNSON

Baseball pitcher Randy Johnson always eats pancakes before a game.

"Some of mankind's most terrible misdeeds have been committed under the spell of certain magic words or phrases." –JAMES BRYANT CONANT

GYPSY CURSE

On October 6, 1997, the London *Daily Mirror* reported the football club in Middleborough had requested the services of psychic Uri Geller to reverse a Gypsy curse. The football club's grounds had been built on a traditional Gypsy camp, and the retaliation was simple: a ritual curse. The club reportedly suffered from continuous bad luck. It is unknown if the reversal worked.

⟨ THE CURSE OF JAMES DEAN'S PORSCHE ⟩

Disaster may be ahead for anyone connected with James Dean's "death car." In 1955, Dean smashed his red Porsche into another car and was killed. The wreckage was bought by George Barris, a friend of Dean's (and the man who customized cars like the Munster's coffinmobile for Hollywood). Barris immediately noticed weird things happening with the car.

First, while being unloaded from the truck that delivered it to Barris, the car slipped and broke a mechanic's legs. Barris then put the car's engine into a race car. The race car crashed in a race, killing the driver. A second car from the same race was equipped with the Porsche's drive shaft; it overturned and injured its driver.

Meanwhile, the shell of the Porsche was being used in a highway-safety display in San Francisco. It fell off its pedestal and broke a teenager's hip. Later, a truck carrying the display to another demonstration was involved in an accident. "The truck driver," says one account, "was thrown out of the cab of the truck and killed when the Porsche shell rolled off the back of the truck and crushed him."

In 1960, the Porsche finally vanished—while on a train en route to Los Angeles.

⟨ THE PRESIDENTIAL DEATH CYCLE ⟩

Between 1840 and 1960, every U.S. president elected in a year ending in zero either died in office of natural causes or was assassinated. By contrast, since 1840, of the twenty-nine presidents who were *not* elected in years ending with a zero, only one has died in office and not one has been assassinated.

The first president to die in office was William Henry Harrison, elected in 1840. Other victims were Abraham Lincoln, elected in 1860 and fatally shot in 1865; James Garfield, elected in 1880 and assassinated in 1881; William McKinley, reelected in 1900 and fatally shot in 1901; Franklin D. Roosevelt, elected for the third time in 1940 and died in 1945; and John F. Kennedy, elected in 1960 and assassinated in 1963.

Ronald Reagan, elected in 1980, was nearly the eighth victim; he was shot and badly wounded by John Hinckley in 1983. Astrologers insist that Reagan was exempted from the "curse" because 1980 included an astrological aberration: Jupiter and Saturn met in an air sign, Libra. They say whether or not the curse is actually over remains to be seen. The next potential victim will be the president elected in 2020.

⟨ THE CURSE OF THE INCAN MUMMY ⟩

Three Andean mummies were discovered by an archaeologist/mountaineer in October 1995. They had been undisturbed in snow at the top of 20,000-foot Mount Ampato, in southern Peru, for at least 500 years. Then an earthquake exposed them. One of the mummies was the remains of a young woman, referred to by local shamans as Juanita. She had apparently been sacrificed to Incan gods.

By disturbing the remains, the authorities are said to have brought bad luck to the Peruvian region. Within a year of the discovery, a Peruvian commercial jet crashed and killed 123 people near the discovery site. Then thirty-five people were electrocuted when a high-tension cable fell on a crowd celebrating the founding of the city of Arequipa (which also is near the discovery site).

Local shamans said these deadly disasters were the acts of the angered ice princess. To break the curse, the shamans gathered in the city of Arequipa in August 1996 and chanted: "Juanita, calm your ire. Do not continue to damn innocent people who have done nothing to you." Apparently, it worked—no deadly accidents have been reported in the region since 1996.

⟨ THE CURSE OF TOSCA ⟩

Productions of Giacomo Puccini's opera *Tosca* have been plagued with problems at least as far back as the 1920s, when, during a production at the Metropolitan Opera, the prop knife with which the heroine Tosca murders the villain Scarpia at the end of act II failed to retract. Singer Antonio Scotti was stabbed. In 1965, at Covent Gardens, Maria Callas's hair caught fire while she was singing the title role. The flames had to be put out by a quick-thinking Tito Gobbi, who was playing Scarpia. Then, in a production in Rome that same year, Gianni Raimondi's face was scorched during the firing-squad scene in act III. In 1993, Elisabeth Knighton Printy, in the scene in which Tosca commits suicide by leaping from a building, jumped off the wrong side of the stage in St. Paul, Minnesota, and plunged more than thirty feet to the ground, breaking both her legs.

The last reported incident was in 1995, when Fabio Armitliatu, starring in a Roman production, was hit in the leg by debris from blanks fired in the act III execution scene. He was taken off the stage on a stretcher. Two weeks later, he returned to the stage and fell and broke his other leg in two places while standing in the wings at the end of the first act.

⊰ THE *SPORTS ILLUSTRATED* JINX ⊱

For decades, sports stars have claimed that appearing on the cover of *Sports Illustrated* magazine was the fastest way to a slump or defeat.

Studying the records of fifty-eight baseball players going back to 1955, researchers found that there was a tendency for players' batting performances to decline, by about fifty points, from the time immediately before they get on the magazine cover until three weeks after the appearance.

Scientists say that if there is anything to this jinx, it's only because it spooks players and thus is self-fulfilling. Because being on the cover of a magazine draws attention to the player, he begins to feel self-conscious at the plate and focus more effort on his performance. That self-consciousness and extra effort might, in turn, cause more injuries, fatigue, or other interruptions in the hitter's natural performance. As a result, his performance suffers.

⊰ THE OSCAR CURSE ⊱

Winning the much-coveted gold statuette can ruin, rather than help, an actor's career. It started when Luise

Rainer won back-to-back Oscars for *The Great Ziegfeld* (1936) and *The Good Earth* (1937). Two years and five terrible movies later, she was considered a has-been. Hollywood columnist Louella Parsons wrote that Rainer was suffering from the "Oscar curse."

Rita Moreno and George Chakiris (1961's best supporting actress and actor, for *West Side Story*) disappeared from films after winning. Richard Dreyfuss, who won best actor in 1978 for *The Goodbye Girl*, raised his weight to 180 pounds, stopped bathing, and started binging on booze and drugs after he won. Michael Cimino, the winner for best director in 1978 for *The Deer Hunter*, followed his Oscar with three unsuccessful films: *Heaven's Gate*, *Year of the Dragon*, and *The Sicilian* Linda Hunt won best supporting actress in 1983 for *The Year of Living Dangerously* and was last seen in the short-lived sci-fi TV series, *Space Rangers*.

This curse is considered quite credible in Hollywood. Oscars are accompanied by high expectations that can't always be fulfilled. The curse can also be attributed to winners' increased salary demands, typecasting, greedy agents or studio bosses, and stars who believe their own press and become hard to work with.

THE BOOK OF THE BIZARRE

⟨ THE CURSE OF LADY TICHBORNE ⟩

In the year 1150, the saintly Lady Mabella Tichborne lay dying in her room at Tichborne Manor in England. For months she had lacked the strength to even sit by her window and overlook her beautiful rich farmland. She summoned her husband, Sir Roger de Tichborne, and shared with him her dying wish: that a loaf of bread be given to all the poor once a year on Lady Day, a feast day of the Virgin Mary.

But greedy Sir Roger felt no compassion toward the hungry and poor, and he quickly schemed to put an end to her request. He told his wife that he would distribute an annual gift in her name, equal to the amount of land she could walk upon holding a lighted torch. Assured that she couldn't get out of bed, Sir Roger was certain that he had settled the matter.

But Lady Mabella surprised him. She crawled out of bed, took the torch, and dragged her body around twenty-three acres of their estate. (To this day, this parcel of land is known as the Crawls.)

Back in her bed, Lady Mabella gathered the household around her and uttered the Tichborne curse. If the yearly dole of bread was ever stopped, the Tichborne family would die out.

So began the Tichborne dole. The custom went on for 600 years, until the local government got fed up with the influx of riffraff that showed up for it and shut it down in 1794. Afterward, male Tichborne heirs began to die.

Edward Doughty, a Tichborne ancestor who had changed his name, realized that the curse was in action when four of his brothers died without children. With the sudden death of his six-year-old son—the only remaining Tichborne heir—he reinstated the dole, which has been handed out ever since.

⟨ THE CURSE OF THE SCREAMING SKULL ⟩

During the seventeenth century, Azariah Pinney, a resident of Bettiscombe, a town in the heart of the English countryside, returned home after living in the West Indies for quite some time. Pinney brought a slave home with him to help care for his house, known as Bettiscombe Manor. The slave, unfortunately, soon fell ill, and lying upon his deathbed, requested one thing from his master. He asked that his corpse be sent home and buried in the land of his birth. Pinney agreed, but when the slave passed away, he broke the promise and buried the slave in a nearby church cemetery.

Immediately after the burial, a strange moaning drifted up through the earth under which the slave had been buried. Before long, the moaning turned into an endless and agonizing scream, which tore through the countryside. Upon finding out about Pinney's broken promise, the local villagers demanded that he immediately dig up the body and remove it from the cemetery. Pinney did as told, and returned with the body to Bettiscombe Manor, where he stored the body in the attic. The tortured screams ceased. The corpse remained in Pinney's house, where it decayed over time, until all that remained was the skull.

As the years passed, Bettiscombe Manor saw many owners come and go. Some did not take well to sleeping so near the infamous skull and made the mistake of removing it from the attic. One owner threw the skull into a nearby pond, thinking it would sink, but the skull rose to the surface shrieking in anguish. Another family buried it in the backyard garden, but it dug itself out of the ground. In the end, the skull was returned to the house, where it is said to reside peacefully to this day.

⟨ THE CURSE OF KING TUT'S TOMB ⟩

For centuries, thieves broke into the tombs in Egypt's Valley of the Kings and ran off with gold and treasures. Modern-day archaeologist Howard Carter was certain that one untouched tomb remained undiscovered and untouched: the tomb of King Tutankhamen, a mysterious pharaoh who had died at the age of eighteen. For thirty years, Carter was obsessed with finding the king's tomb, but by 1922, he felt like his luck was running out. Carter's digs had been funded by his friend Lord Carnarvon, who was losing a fortune and didn't want to spend anymore. But Carter begged for one more dig, and he got the funds for it. He began digging in the last unexplored part of the valley, and in November 1922 uncovered a descending staircase. Excited beyond belief, Carter called his benefactor and had him join him immediately.

On November 26, 1922, Carter scraped a hole through the doorway to King Tut's tomb. Over the next few days Carter and Carnarvon broke through the sealed doors and found rooms filled with gold statues, furniture, jewelry, and other invaluable objects. They also found a frightening message on a clay tablet: "Death will slay with his wings whoever disturbs the peace of the pharaoh." Fearing that the Egyptian workers who were with them would flee if they saw the inscription, the two men hid the tablet away.

King Tut's tomb soon proved to be the greatest archaeological discovery of all time. The curse—which reached the newspapers after Carnarvon sold the story—became the most famous in history as headlines around the world announced, "the Curse of the Pharaohs."

The curse's first victim was Lord Carnarvon, who died of an unknown disease just five months after the discovery of the tomb. An American journalist who had helped unseal the tomb fell into a coma and died shortly after Carnarvon. A friend of Carnarvon's, who had come to visit the tomb, died the next day. A radiologist who took x-rays of King Tut's mummy died after returning to England. The death toll continued to climb, and by 1929 the curse had been credited with claiming twenty-two lives. Oddly enough, archaeologist Howard Carter survived the curse and died of natural causes in 1939, at the age of sixty-four.

⟨ THE CURSE OF THE *HINEMOA* ⟩

The ship *Hinemoa* was named after the beautiful daughter of a very powerful New Zealand chief. In 1892, the ship set sail on the first voyage of what would become a chilling history of terror. A string of bad luck for its first captains revealed that something was very, very wrong with the steamer. The first captain went insane and had to be replaced. The second captain fell victim to foul play and was thrown into prison. The third became a drunk and, shaking from d.t.'s, lost his job. Captain four mysteriously died in his cabin, and the captain of the fifth voyage committed suicide.

The next time the *Hinemoa* set sail, it lost its balance and turned over. Righted again, it went to sea once more and put its curse on two sailors, who were washed overboard into the Pacific during the trip.

This terrible and ghastly curse continued until the last voyage of the *Hinemoa* in September 1917, when it crossed paths with a deadly German submarine. Shortly thereafter, the *Hinemoa* sank, bringing the curse to a watery end.

The *Hinemoa*'s faithful crew knew why the ship was cursed. They claimed that deadly forces entered the ship when it was being built and were stored up in the vessel's "heart." How did these forces arrive and in what form? The first ballast—heavy material used to give the ship stability—was gravel from a London graveyard.

13. THE DARK SIDE OF THE MOON

UFO STORIES AND BIZARRE AND TRUE LUNAR FACTS

⟨ ROSWELL: WHAT HAPPENED? ⟩

William "Mac" Brazel was working as a foreman on the Foster ranch seventy miles north of Roswell, New Mexico, when reports about sightings of "flying discs" started circulating in the news and among locals. Weeks before, on June 14, 1947, Brazel had noticed some strange and suspicious debris on the property. He reported to the Roswell *Daily Record* that he and his son spotted a "large area of bright wreckage made up of rubber strips, tinfoil, a rather tough paper and sticks," but that he didn't return to the wreckage until he connected the stories of the flying discs to the material he had found. The timing of the incident is controversial, but some contemporary accounts suggest that Brazel returned to the site with Air Force Major Jesse Marcel and some plainclothes officers on July 6. As the story goes, the officials collected the debris, which they claimed was the remains of a weather balloon. The subsequent investigation, which involved the FBI, was reportedly classified.

The story of UFOs in Roswell, New Mexico, would have probably stayed dead if Stanton T. Friedman, a nuclear physicist, hadn't lost his job during the 1970s. UFOs were Friedman's hobby, and soon after his termination, they became his career. He became a full-time lecturer. He delivered his favorite talk, titled, "Flying Saucers *Are* Real," at more than 600 different college campuses and other venues around the country.

Friedman soon developed a nationwide reputation as a UFO expert, and people who'd seen UFOs began seeking him out. In 1978, Jesse Marcel, the U.S. Army intelligence officer who'd retrieved the wreckage from Mac Brazel's ranch thirty-one years earlier, even made contact with him. Friedman urged Marcel to give an interview to the *National Enquirer*, which he did, explaining that what he had picked up from the ranch was indeed not of this earth.

The interview couldn't have come at a better time: it was published in 1979, and Steven Spielberg's film *Close Encounters of the Third Kind* had just premiered, stoking the public's appetite for UFO stories. After thirty years, the Roswell story blew up once again, and since that time the story just kept on growing. New "witnesses" to the Roswell UFO began seeking out Friedman to tell him their stories. Soon, the Roswell story included humanoid alien beings. (For the record, neither Mac Brazel nor Jesse Marcel ever claimed to have seen aliens among the wreckage. No one went public with those claims until more than thirty years after the fact.)

So was the U.S. government hiding evidence of an alien crash-landing on earth? In 1993, Congressman Steven Schiff of New Mexico asked the U.S. General Accounting Office to look into whether the government had ever been involved in a space-alien cover-up, either in Roswell, New Mexico, or anyplace else. The GAO spent eighteen months searching government archives dating back to the 1940s, including even the highly classified minutes of the National Security Council. The GAO's research also prompted the U.S. Air Force to launch its own investigation. It released its findings in September 1994, and the GAO's report followed in November 1995.

The reports arrived at the same conclusion. What the conspiracy theorists believe were UFOs were actually products of top-secret research programs run by the U.S. military during the Cold War. According to the reports, the object that crashed on Brazel's farm in Roswell was a balloon, but not just any balloon—it was part of Project Mogul, a secret defense program geared toward detecting nuclear weapons exploded by the Soviets. In the late 1940s, the U.S. had neither spy satellites nor high-altitude spy planes that it could send over the Soviet Union to see if they were succeeding at building nuclear weapons. Government scientists figured weather balloons fitted with special sensing equipment, if launched high enough into the atmosphere, might be able to detect the shock waves given off by nuclear explosions thousands of miles away.

The Roswell intelligence officers who recovered the wreckage didn't have high enough security clearance to know about Project Mogul, and thus they didn't know to inform anyone of the discovery. On the whole, Project Mogul was successful. Apparently, the equipment it generated did detect the first Soviet nuclear blasts.

The air force's 1994 report suggested that a number of other military projects that took place in the 1940s and 1950s had become part of the Roswell myth as well. In the 1950s, the air force launched balloons as high as nineteen miles into the atmosphere and dropped human dummies to test parachutes for pilots of the X-15 rocket plane and the U-2 spy plane. The dummies, the air force says, were sometimes mistaken for aliens; because it didn't want the real purpose of the tests to be revealed, it did not debunk the alien theories. Some balloons also dropped mock interplanetary probes, which looked a lot like flying saucers. In one particular crash, a serviceman named Captain Dan D. Fulgham, crashed a test balloon ten miles northwest of Roswell and suffered an injury that caused his head to swell considerably.

The incident, the air force says, helped inspire the notion that aliens have large heads.

Have these reports deterred conspiracy theorists? Obviously not all of them have. Who knows what really happened, and whom we can trust?

※※

➤ Ufology, the study of UFO evidence, was invented during the late 1970s when investigators interviewed people who worked at or near Roswell. Ufology is now part of our popular culture.

➤ The thirty-year-old Committee for the Scientific Investigation of the Paranormal (CSICOP) opines that UFO sightings are hallucinations.

※※

⟨ FIRST UFO SIGHTING ⟩

In 1947, less than a month before the incident at Roswell, New Mexico, Kenneth Arnold, a pilot from Boise, Idaho, reported seeing nine unusual objects in the sky near Mount Rainier. He described the mysterious objects as "bright" and said they were flying at a "tremendous speed." His experience is said to be the first sighting of unidentified flying objects (UFOs). In

1952, Arnold wrote and self-published *The Coming of the Saucers*, the first UFO book.

> "THOSE WHO DREAM BY DAY ARE COGNIZANT OF MANY THINGS THAT ESCAPE THOSE WHO DREAM ONLY AT NIGHT." —EDGAR ALLAN POE

⟨ UFO RELIGIONS ⟩

UFOs are major components of some new religions, including Unarius, the Aetherians, the Order of the Solar Temple (whose believers thought they would be carried away by the Hale-Bopp comet), the Raelians, and Scientology (whose mythos tells of a galactic emperor who brought billions of people to earth and killed them). The UFO religions, which tend to be apocalyptic, profess a belief in superior beings (the old gods?) who will come down from the sky and save the true believers.

"The fancy that extraterrestrial life is by definition of a higher order than our own is one that soothes all children, and many writers." –JOAN DIDION

According to a 2005 Gallup poll, 24 percent of Americans and 19 percent of Britons believe that extraterrestrials have visited earth at some time in the past. Men are more receptive to the idea of alien visits than women are.

⟨ IF YOU'VE BEEN ABDUCTED . . . ⟩

Each alien abduction story is different, but there are key elements to almost every one. Most people who claim to have been abducted describe combinations of the following:

➢ Light, often from a beam that sucks the person into the spacecraft;

➢ A disk-shaped spacecraft that looks very high tech;

➢ Medical testing and experimentation, often quite invasive;

➢ "Lost time," or amnesia about a certain period of time.

THE TUNGUSKA EVENT: ⟨ A UFO CRASH LANDING? ⟩

On June 30, 1908, an explosion at or above the Tunguska River in Siberia felled sixty million trees.

When the Soviet government funded an investigation in the 1920s, Leonid Kulik and his associates interviewed eyewitnesses who said they had seen a huge fireball crossing the sky. The blast was estimated to be between ten and fifteen megatons and left an enormous, butterfly-shaped region of scorched and flattened trees.

What was it that exploded? An extraterrestrial body?

In 1930, a British astronomer proposed that it was a small comet. But in 1983, an astronomer at NASA's Jet Propulsion Laboratory wrote that comets are made of ice and dust and that a comet could not have flown so close to the earth without disintegrating. Expeditions sent to the Tunguska River region in the 1950s and 1960s found microscopic glass spheres containing nickel and iridium, which are found in meteorites, and in 2001, investigators suggested the blast was the explosion of a meteorite from the asteroid belt. But there's no typical meteorite crater in the area.

Other theories suggest that a small black hole was passing through the earth, a piece of antimatter exploded, or a nuclear-powered UFO blew up. Some blame Nikola Tesla. In an article written in 1908, Tesla claimed that he could direct electromagnetic-wave energy to any point on earth from his transformer at Wardenclyffe Tower in Shoreham, New York. One of Tesla's associates reported that during one test the Wardenclyffe Tower glowed and an owl flying nearby disintegrated. That's when Tesla stopped talking about projecting electromagnetic force.

To this day, no one knows for sure. *Star Trek*'s explanation is as good as any: An alien race saved humanity by exploding its planet and deflecting an incoming meteor that would have struck Europe. The remnants of the explosion hit Siberia.

⟨ MARFA MYSTERY ⟩

If you're ever driving through Texas and have some time on your hands, travel east from Marfa on U.S. Route 90 to the Mystery Lights Viewing Area, where you can witness Marfa's mysterious white-lights show. According to testimony, the lights flash one at a time, quickly fade away, and then reappear for the public's viewing delight. Are the lights reflections from stars, cars, or city lights? Spaceship high-beams? Astral glow-worms? Nobody knows for sure.

⟨ THE GRAYS ⟩

"Gray" is the term used to describe over 75 percent of aliens sighted in the United States. Grays are typically four to six feet tall and have light gray skin, amorphous bodies with short legs and elongated torsos, and lidless, bulbous eyes. Grays are sometimes known as Roswell aliens, Zetas, or Reticulians, and they are the protagonists in most modern-day UFO conspiracy theories and stories.

In 1948, military pilots and government officials in the New Mexico desert reported seeing strange green orbs floating in the sky. The orbs weren't the result of any secret military testing, officials confirmed, and they did not appear to be meteorites. Some people suggested that the green lights, which resembled pale green flares, were the result of extraterrestrial weaponry testing. A program called Project Twinkle was established to inspect the origins of the lights, but its results were not conclusive, and it was shut down in 1951.

⟨ THE ABDUCTION OF BETTY ANDREASSON ⟩

In 1967, Massachusetts housewife and mother of seven Betty Andreasson went public with her claims that she and members of her family were in regular contact with extraterrestrials. Among her many detailed stories was an incredible account of boarding an alien spacecraft and undergoing medical experiments at the hands of the extraterrestrials. A devout Christian, Andreasson was taken seriously by many in the UFO community because it was thought that such a religious person would not spin tall tales, especially concerning aliens and strange medical procedures. But alas, in 2007 Andreasson's stepson alleged that his mother's stories were untrue and all part of an elaborate hoax to gain money and fame.

When questioned about the nature of the UFOs sighted in Texas in January 2008, a witness claimed the spacecraft was "bigger than a Wal-Mart."

⊰ FOO FIGHTERS ⊱

During World War II, both Axis and Allied fighter pilots reported seeing globes of colored light streaking through in the night sky. Everyone had a name for them; Americans called them foo fighters, a nickname based on a saying from a comic strip character: "Where there's foo, there's fire." The mysterious foo fighters were said to fly in formation with great speed and precision.

⊰ THE MYSTERIOUS FACE OF MARS ⊱

In 1978, NASA's Viking 2 spacecraft was wandering around on Mars, taking pictures of the planet's craggy surface and transmitting them back to earth. Mission controllers watching the camera's movement spotted what resembled a huge, mile-long human face carved into the red rock. The image of the face, with shadows giving the illusion of a nose, mouth, and eyes, was released to the American public days later to great excitement and fanfare. Was there intelligent life on Mars? Was the face some sort of message to humans, left for us to find by crafty aliens?

⊰ A UFO AT O'HARE? ⊱

On November 7, 2006, employees at O'Hare International Airport in Chicago reported an "unidentified object" hovering over gate C17. Multiple witnesses described a small aircraft that whirred in place for a second and then quickly darted east and disappeared. According to reports, it resembled a small metallic

Frisbee and had no lights or identifying marks. The National UFO Reporting Center's report quoted another witness: "All employees are very familiar with aircraft around the world's busiest airport—this was nothing we are familiar with. As a side note as it is probably unrelated, the next aircraft into that gate was experiencing electrical problems."

- The U.K.'s first official study of UFOs, commissioned by the Ministry of Defence in 1950, was called the Flying Saucer Working Party, or FSWP. Writer Nick Pope deemed it "arguably the most marvellously named committee in the history of the civil service."
- Novelist Whitley Strieber, author of *Communion* and *Transformation* and self-proclaimed abduction survivor, believes that aliens exist to help humans grow spiritually.

"MOONLIGHT IS SCULPTURE; SUNLIGHT IS PAINTING."
—NATHANIEL HAWTHORNE

⟨ DID YOU KNOW . . . ? ⟩

- It takes 29 days, 12 hours, 44 minutes, and 3 seconds for the moon to go through all of its phases, from one full moon to the next. This time period is close to the length of a month—which is why the word "month" is derived from the Old English word for "moon."

- The light that comes from the moon is sunlight reflected off the moon's surface. It takes $1\frac{1}{4}$ seconds for the light to travel to earth.

- The moon only reflects 7 percent of the light it receives from the sun.

- The moon is smaller than any planet in the solar system, but relative to the size of the planets they orbit, our moon is the largest of any planet's moons.

- The moon is 2,160 miles in diameter—about a quarter of the earth's diameter. If the earth were as big as a fist, the moon would be the size of a stamp—placed ten feet away.

- The average temperature on the moon is minus 283 degrees to minus 266 degrees Fahrenheit.

- Since the moon spins once on its axis every $27\frac{1}{3}$ days—the same amount of time it takes to go around the earth once—we end up seeing only one side of the moon (about 59 percent of its surface).

- The side of the moon we always see is called the near side. The side we never see from earth is the far side. (That's probably where cartoonist Gary Larsen got the name for the comic strip.)
- There is no sound on the moon. Nor are there weather, wind, clouds, or colors at sunrise and sunset.
- If you weigh 120 pounds on earth, you would weigh 20 pounds—or $\frac{1}{6}$ of your earth weight—on the moon.
- A 3-foot jump on earth would carry you 18 feet, 9 inches, on the moon!
- Astronauts have brought over 843 pounds of moon samples back to earth.
- The moon is moving away from the earth at a rate of about $\frac{1}{8}$ inch a year.

> **"THE MOON WAS A GHOSTLY GALLEON TOSSED UPON CLOUDY SEAS."** —ALFRED NOYES

⟨ ONCE IN A BLUE MOON ⟩

Where does the expression "once in a blue moon" come from? And what does the song "Blue Moon" refer to?

According to the *Dictionary of Word and Phrase Origins*, the term "blue moon" first appeared in England in 1528. The source was a book entitled *Read Me and Be Not Wroth*, which said, "If they say the mone is blew/We must believe that it is true."

The term "once in a blue moon" was apparently derived from this sarcastic little rhyme about the upper class. The phrase originally meant "never," but by the early 1800s it was used to describe a very rare occurrence. This meaning is actually more correct, because two kinds of blue moons really do exist. The phenomenon of a blue moon is associated with unusual atmospheric conditions—a blue moon, or a green one, is most likely to be seen just before sunrise or just after sunset if there is a large quantity of dust or smoke in the atmosphere. The dust or smoke particles can filter out colors like red and yellow, leaving only green and blue to color the moon.

⟨ BLUE MOON ⟩

A modern definition of the term "blue moon" says it is the second full moon that in a calendar month. Double full moon months occur every thirty-two months or so, so clearly they are not a usual occurrence. A blue moon appeared on June 30, 2007, and will also appear on December 31, 2009, and August 31, 2012.

Another definition of a blue moon says it is the third full moon in a season that has four full moons. In order to set the date for Easter Sunday properly, the medieval ecclesiastic calendar required a maximum of twelve full moons during the year; by calling the occasional thirteenth full moon a blue moon—meaning it didn't really count—the calendar was kept on track.

Saying the moon is blue, serious people tell us, is like saying it is made of green cheese. But with air pollution, clouds, and ice crystals in the atmosphere, the moon does occasionally appear to be blue.

⟨ MOON GODS ⟩

In many ancient cultures, the sun was seen as a god and the moon as a goddess. The sun's energy is projective. Daytime is more important than nighttime. Sun gods are strong and creative; moon goddesses are mystical and mysterious.

But to some European cultures, the sun was female and the moon was male. In the far-northern European countries, where the sun shone little or not at all during the winter months, the spring sun was welcomed as a nurturing, generating, creative—and therefore feminine—force.

The so-called man in the moon first appeared in a Saxon folktale with his wife, the woman in the sun. Earlier, the Sumerian city Ur was named after the moon god Hur. The Babylonian moon god, Sin, was known as the father of time. His name is a contraction of the Sumerian words "Su" and "En," meaning "the crescent moon." Also called Nanna ("the full moon"), Sin was the father of Ishtar. The latter is said to have been the source of the voice that spoke to the Hebrew leader Moses from the famous burning bush, the divine presence on Mount Sinai, and the carver of commandments. In Iran, 4,500 years ago, the moon was worshipped as the Great Man, who incarnated on earth as a divine ruler. Even the great thirteenth-century Mongol emperor Genghis Khan traced his ancestry back to a moon god.

The moon gods were overthrown by the sun and sky gods. Solar gods married solar goddesses and usurped the moon gods' mythologies. Conquering tribal chiefs married female shamans and stole their powers. Men mastered the horse, fire, and metallurgy, and built cities and temples. It is said that men came to fear what they couldn't see in broad daylight, under the blazing sun, so they relegated the mysteries of the night to something else they feared—woman.

❉❉❉❉❉❉❉❉❉❉❉❉❉❉❉❉❉❉❉❉❉❉❉❉❉❉❉❉❉❉❉❉❉❉❉❉❉❉

➤ UCLA astronomer Andrea Ghez has observed super-massive black holes at the center of the Milky Way and has posited that most, if not all, galaxies have similar black holes at their cores. These cosmic giants can eat stars whole, and the one at the center of our galaxy is said to have the mass of forty suns.

➤ Every 100,000 years the earth's orbital path goes from circular to almost elliptical, altering the distance between the earth and the sun.

➤ Every 42,000 years the earth's tilt alters and changes the area exposed directly to the sun.

➤ Every 25,800 years the earth wobbles, causing solstices and equinoxes to move.

❉❉❉❉❉❉❉❉❉❉❉❉❉❉❉❉❉❉❉❉❉❉❉❉❉❉❉❉❉❉❉❉❉❉❉❉❉❉

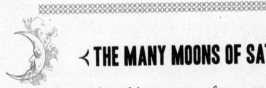

⟨ THE MANY MOONS OF SATURN ⟩

Saturn has thirty moons—far more than any other planet. It has so many that half of them have numbers for names: Pan, Atlas, Prometheus, Pandora, Epimetheus, Janus, Mimas, Enceladus, Tethys, Telesto,

Calypso, Dione, Helene, Rhea, Titan, Hyperion, Iapetus, Phoebe, S/2000 S 1, S/2000 S 2, S/2000 S 3, S/2000 S 4, S/2000 S 5, S/2000 S 6, S/2000 S 7, S/2000 S 8, S/2000 S 9, S/2000 S 10, S/2000 S 11, and S/2000 S 12.

⊰ THE RARE EARLY EASTER SUNDAY ⊱

The date of the Christian Easter celebration is always the first Sunday after the first full moon after the vernal equinox (March 21). This schedule is based on the lunar calendar that Hebrew people used to identify Passover, which is why Easter Sunday moves around on the Gregorian calendar used in the United States and other Western countries today.

Based on this formula, Easter will never fall before March 22 or after April 25.

In 2008, Easter Sunday fall on March 23, making the earliest Easter most people will ever observe in their entire lives. The last time Easter fell that early in the year was in 1913; that means anyone age ninety-five or older in 2008 are the only people who have witnessed this exceptionally early Easter twice in their lives. It is extremely unlikely that anyone alive in 2008 will live to see another such early Easter, because the next time Easter will fall on March 23 will be in the year 2160.

No one alive today has seen, and likely ever will see, Easter Sunday fall earlier than March 23. The last time it did so was in 1818, when it fell on March 22, and it won't fall on that date again until the year 2285.

"There is something haunting in the light of the moon; it has all the dispassionateness of a disembodied soul, and something of its inconceivable mystery." –JOSEPH CONRAD

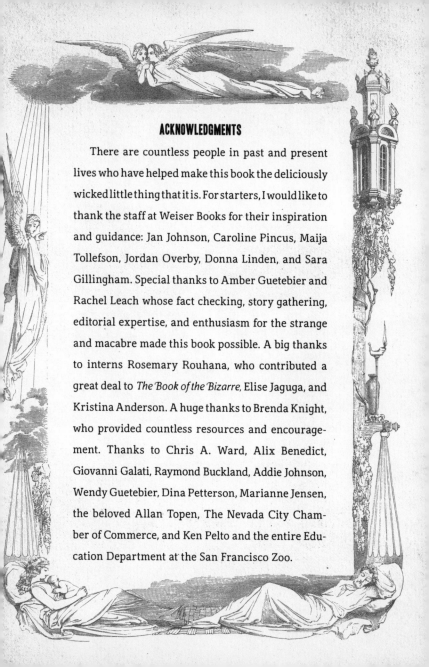

ACKNOWLEDGMENTS

There are countless people in past and present lives who have helped make this book the deliciously wicked little thing that it is. For starters, I would like to thank the staff at Weiser Books for their inspiration and guidance: Jan Johnson, Caroline Pincus, Maija Tollefson, Jordan Overby, Donna Linden, and Sara Gillingham. Special thanks to Amber Guetebier and Rachel Leach whose fact checking, story gathering, editorial expertise, and enthusiasm for the strange and macabre made this book possible. A big thanks to interns Rosemary Rouhana, who contributed a great deal to *The Book of the Bizarre*, Elise Jaguga, and Kristina Anderson. A huge thanks to Brenda Knight, who provided countless resources and encouragement. Thanks to Chris A. Ward, Alix Benedict, Giovanni Galati, Raymond Buckland, Addie Johnson, Wendy Guetebier, Dina Petterson, Marianne Jensen, the beloved Allan Topen, The Nevada City Chamber of Commerce, and Ken Pelto and the entire Education Department at the San Francisco Zoo.

BIBLIOGRAPHY

BOOKS

Adams, Norman. *Scottish Bodysnatchers*. Musselburgh, Scotland: Goblinshead, 2002.

Allen, Judy. *Unexplained: An Encyclopedia of Curious Phenomena, Strange Superstitions, and Ancient Mysteries*. Boston: Kingfisher, 2006.

Alvrez, Alicia. *The Big Book of Women's Trivia*. San Francisco: Conari Press, 2007.

Ascalone, Enrico. *Mesopotamia*. Berkeley: University of California Press, 2005.

Austin, Joanne. *Weird Hauntings*. New York: Sterling, 2006.

Ballenger, Seale. *Hell's Belles*. Berkeley, CA: Conari Press, 1997.

Barrett, Erin, and Jack Mingo. *Al Capone Was a Golfer*. Boston: Conari Press, 2002.

———. *Cats Don't Always Land on Their Feet*. Boston: Conari Press, 2002.

———. *Dracula Was a Lawyer*. Boston: Conari Press, 2002.

———. *It Takes a Certain Type to Be a Writer*. Boston: Conari Press, 2002.

———. *Just Curious About History, Jeeves*. New York: Pocket Books, 2002.

———. *Not Another Apple for the Teacher*. Boston: Conari Press, 2002.

———. *Random Kinds of Factness*. San Francisco: Conari Press, 2005.

Belanger, Jeff. *Communicating With the Dead*. Franklin Lake, NJ: New Page Books, 2005.

———. *The Encyclopedia of Haunted Places*. Franklin Lake, NJ: New Page Books, 2005.

Book of Secrets. Kansas City: Andrews McMeel, 2005.

Brewer, E. Cobham. *Brewer's Dictionary of Phrase and Fable*. New York: Harper & Row, 1970.

Budapest, Zsuzsanna Emese. *The Holy Book of Women's Mysteries*. San Francisco: Weiser Books, 2007.

Cheetham, Erika. *The Prophecies of Nostradamus*. New York: Perigee Books, 1973.

Colman, Penny. *Corpses, Coffins, and Crypts*. New York: Henry Holt and Co., 1997.

Cooper, Patrinella. *Gypsy Magic*. Boston: Weiser Books, 2002.

Cousineau, Phil. *Coincidence or Destiny*. Boston: Conari Press, 1997.

Couch, Ernie. *Presidential Trivia*. Nashville: Rutledge Hill Press, 1996.

Coulombe, Charles A. *Haunted Castles of the World*. Guilford, CT: Lyons Press, 2004.

DuQuette, Lon Milo. *The Book of Ordinary Oracles*. Boston: Weiser Books, 2005.

Dwyer, Jeff. *Ghost Hunters Guide to the San Francisco Bay Area*. Gretna, LA: Pelican Publishing, 2005.

Eaton, Thomas. *Book of Secrets*. Kansas City: Andrews McMeel, 2005.

Fei, Alberto Toso. *Venetian Legends and Ghost Stories*. Treviso, Italy: Elzeviro, 2002.

Ferguson, Sibyl. *Crystal Ball*. Boston: Weiser Books, 2005.

Fiedler, Leslie. *Freaks*. New York: Simon & Schuster, 1978.

Gabucci, Ada. *Rome*. Berkeley: University of California Press, 2005.

Guiley, Rosemary Ellen. *Harper's Encyclopedia of Mystical & Paranormal Experience*. San Francisco: HarperSanFrancisco, 1991.

Illes, Judika. *Pure Magic*. San Francisco: Weiser Books, 2007

Keister, Douglas. *Stories in Stone: A Field Guide to Cemetery Symbolism and Iconography*. Salt Lake City: Gibbs Smith, 2004.

Kipfer, Barbara Ann. *How It Happens*. New York: Random House, 2005.

Lachenmeyer, Nathaniel. *13*. New York: Thunder's Mouth Press, 2004.

Largo, Michael. *Final Exits*. New York: Harper Collins, 2006.

Lyndoe, Edward. *Everybody's Book of Fate and Fortune*. New York: Wise & Co., 1938.

McKenna, Terence. *The Archaic Revival*. San Francisco: HarperSanFrancisco, 1991.

Moran, Mark, and Mark Sceurman. *Weird U.S.* New York: Barnes & Noble Books, 2004.

Norman, Michael, and Beth Scott. *Haunted Heritage*. New York: Forge, 2002.

Opie, Iona, and Moira Tatem, eds. *A Dictionary of Superstitions*. New York: Oxford University Press, 1989.

Patterson, R. Gary. *Take A Walk on the Dark Side*. New York: Fireside, 2004.

Podolski, Edward, ed. *Encyclopedia of Aberrations*. New York: Citadel Press, 1953.

Pearson, Mike Parker. *The Archaeology of Death and Burial*. Gloucestershire, England: Sutton Publishing Limited, 1999.

Richards, Rand. *Haunted San Francisco*. San Francisco: Heritage House, 2004.

Robbins, Trina. *Tender Murderers*. Boston: Conari Press, 2003.

Rogak, Lisa. *Death Warmed Over*. Berkeley, CA: Ten Speed Press, 2004.

Rule, Leslie. *Coast to Coast Ghosts*. Kansas City: Andrews McMeel, 2001.

Scary Nuns. New York: Harper Collins, 2007.

Shaw, Karl. *Five People Who Died During Sex*. New York: Broadway Books, 2007.

Steiger, Brad. *Real Ghosts, Restless Spirits, and Haunted Places*. Canton, MI: Visible Ink Press, 2003.

Tabori, Lena, and Natasha Tabori Fried. *The Little Big Book of Chills and Thrills*. New York: Welcome Books, 2001.

Ventura, Varla. *Sheroes*. Berkeley, CA: Conari Press, 1998.

Whitworth, Belinda. *The New Age Encyclopedia*. Franklin Lakes, NJ: New Page Books, 2003.

ONLINE SOURCES

about.com

ArcaMax Publishing: News and Features, U.K. News (*arcamax.com/uknews*)

Alternative Reel (*alternativereel.com/*)

BBC News (*bbc.co.uk*)

classicrock.about.com/

corsinet.com

Creative Writing Corner (*blairhurley.com*)

Crystalinks: Elle Crystal's Metaphysical and Science Website (*crystalinks.com*)

Fortean Times (*forteantimes.com*)

Gallop (*Gallup.com*)

IMDb: The Internet Movie Database (*imdb.com*)

National UFO Reporting Center (*nuforc.org*)

The Nevada County Union (*theunion.com*)

The New York Times (*nytimes.com*)

Ripley's Believe It or Not (*Ripleys.com*)

The San Francisco Chronicle (*sfgate.com*)

telegraph.co.uk

Wikipedia: The Free Encyclopedia (*wikipedia.org*)

world-mysteries.com

Yahoo! News (*News.yahoo.com*)